Practicing Social Ecology

"At a time of ecological collapse and rising authoritarianism, when we desperately need new forms of social organization, this lively book provides a wonderfully accessible exposition of the foundational ideas of social ecology—and inspiring examples of its practice. A powerful call to action for all who believe we can, and must, create a more democratic and ecological society."
—Debbie Bookchin, journalist, author,
daughter of Murray Bookchin

"*Practicing Social Ecology* comes at a perfect time for our collective rethinking of how society can, and must, be reorganized so that all life can flourish with autonomy, horizontality, dignity, and deep care. The theories and examples in this book guide us in our rethinking and remaking the world, not as a prescription, and still with translatable and grounded examples."
—Marina Sitrin, Professor of Sociology,
Binghamton University

T0335254

FireWorks

Series editors:

Gargi Bhattacharyya, Director of the Sarah Parker Remond Centre, University College London

Anitra Nelson, Associate Professor, Honorary Principal Fellow, Melbourne Sustainable Society Institute, University of Melbourne

Also available

FireWorks

Practicing Social Ecology

From Bookchin to Rojava and Beyond

Eleanor Finley

First published 2025 by Pluto Press
New Wing, Somerset House, Strand, London WC2R 1LA
and Pluto Press, Inc.
1930 Village Center Circle, 3-834, Las Vegas, NV 89134

www.plutobooks.com

British Library Cataloguing in Publication Data
A catalogue record for this book is available from the British Library

ISBN 978 0 7453 4690 8   Paperback
ISBN 978 0 7453 4694 6   PDF
ISBN 978 0 7453 4692 2   EPUB

This book is printed on paper suitable for recycling and made from
fully managed and sustained forest sources. Logging, pulping and
manufacturing processes are expected to conform to the environmental
standards of the country of origin.

Typeset by Stanford DTP Services, Northampton, England

Simultaneously printed in the United Kingdom and United States of
America

Contents

Figures

Series Preface

Addressing urgent questions about how to make a just and sustainable world, the FireWorks series throws a new light on contemporary movements, crises and challenges. Each book is written to extend the popular imagination and unmake dominant framings of key issues.

Launched in 2020, the series offers guides to matters of social equity, justice and environmental sustainability. FireWorks books provide short, accessible and authoritative commentaries that illuminate underground political currents or marginalised voices, and highlight political thought and writing that exists substantially in languages other than English. Their authors seek to ignite key debates for twenty-first-century politics, economics and society.

FireWorks books do not assume specialist knowledge, but offer up-to-date and well-researched overviews for a wide range of politically-aware readers. They provide an opportunity to go deeper into a subject than is possible in current news and online media, but are still short enough to be read in a few hours.

In these fast-changing times, these books provide snappy and thought-provoking interventions on complex political issues. As times get dark, FireWorks offer a flash of light to reveal the broader social landscape and economic structures that form our political moment.

Glossary

communalism The political dimension of social ecology that promotes federations of directly democratic popular assemblies within free eco-communities.

democratic autonomy The program for autonomous self-governance of southeast Turkey's Kurdish-majority regions advocated by the Kurdish Freedom Movement.

democratic confederalism The political philosophy that promotes federations of popular assemblies, councils, and participatory politics advocated by the Kurdish Freedom Movement.

dialectic A philosophical term meaning change through dialog and differentiation.

dual power The political theory that revolutionaries can win popular legitimacy by building an alternative "counterpower" that provides for people's basic needs better than the existing government.

first nature The dialectical process of natural evolution pertaining to all organic life; includes plants, animals, microorganisms, and humans.

hevaltî The Kurmanji term for friendship by which Kurdish revolutionaries address one another.

hierarchy A system of relationships based on obedience and command, often enforced by the threat of force. It is also a worldview that ranks some people as superior to others.

horizontality A system of relationships based on equality and mutualism. Access to power is distributed evenly among participants within a given institution or organization.

jineoloji A Kurmanji term meaning the science of women and life.

libertarian municipalism Bookchin's proposal for how to build dual power, dissolve nation-states, and reconstitute local municipalities using direct democracy.

municipalism An international movement to democratize city governments and empower citizens through civic platforms, progressive candidates, social service programs, public ownership, and other reforms.

post-scarcity The state at which society has environmentally sustainable technology that is advanced enough to provide for everyone's needs and enable personal and collective choices based on desire rather than necessity.

second nature The dialectical process of social evolution pertaining to the human-made world we live in; includes arts and culture, buildings and infrastructure, technology, traditions, and politics.

social ecology A holistic philosophy based on the idea that nature and society are integrated. Also a social movement that opposes all forms of hierarchy and domination and that advances social and ecological liberation.

third nature An envisioned future stage of evolution that resolves the divide between first nature (the natural world) and second nature (human-created systems and environments).

unity in diversity The social-ecological principle that there is stability in diverse ecosystems; individuals make up the collective and vice versa.

Abbreviations

BDP	Peace and Democracy Party (Barış ve Demokrasi Partisi)
EZLN	Zapatista Army of National Liberation (Ejército Zapatista de Liberación Nacional)
FLN	Forces of National Liberation (Fuerzas de Liberación Nacional)
GMO	genetically modified organism
HDP	People's Democratic Party (Halkların Demokratik Partisi)
IMF	International Monetary Fund
ISE	Institute for Social Ecology
PAH	Platform of Those Affected by Mortgage Debt (Plataforma de los Afectados por la Hipoteca)
PKK	Kurdistan Workers' Party (Partiya Karkerên Kurdistan)
PYD	Democratic Union Party (Partiya Yekîtiya Demokrat)
TEV-DEM	Movement for a Democratic Society (Tevgera Civaka Demokratîk)
YPG	People's Protection Units (Yekîneyên Parastina Gel)
YPJ	Women's Protection Units (Yekîneyên Parastina Jin)
WTO	World Trade Organization

Acknowledgments

I first want to thank the many activists who took the time to be interviewed for this book. Without their hospitality, generosity, solidarity, and practical assistance, this project would not have been possible. Of course, special acknowledgment is due to the close-knit political community of social ecology. Thank you to Dan Chodorkoff, Brian Tokar, Alan Goodman, Peter Staudenmaier, Debbie and Bea Bookchin, Federico Venturini, and many others in and around the Institute for Social Ecology. I especially want to thank Dr Chaia Heller, whose mentorship and feminist consciousness helped me see myself as a revolutionary and scholar. Thank you as well to the institute and to the Bookchin Trust for their photo permissions. I am equally grateful to friends in Kurdish-led and Kurdish solidarity organizations such as Freedom for Öcalan – Peace in Kurdistan, the Civil Diplomacy Center, and the Mesopotamia Ecology Movement. Thank you for sharing your remarkable world so that I could bear witness to history in the making.

The Department of Anthropology at the University of Massachusetts, Amherst, also has my deep gratitude for funding various periods of fieldwork and for providing me with a writing fellowship to complete it. Tremendous thanks to my advisor, Dr. Jacqueline Urla, as well as my doctoral committee and faculty mentors Marina Sitrin and Krista Harper for supporting and encouraging my unconventional scholarship.

Over the years, a great number of friends and colleagues helped make this work possible through their support. My editors at Pluto Press, David Castle and Anitra Nelson, deserve special thanks for their careful feedback, guidance, and patience despite the interference of serious personal setbacks during the drafting of this manuscript. Jesse Cohen, Peter Staudenmaier, Debbie Bookchin, and Dan Chodorkoff helped enormously with edits of drafts, and to them I am truly thankful. Thank you to the teams at Next System Studies, *ROAR Magazine*, and the Institute for Anarchist Studies. Lastly, I want to share deep gratitude to my mother, Sherri, and my partner, Tony, for bringing me joy and providing practical support throughout this process.

Introduction
Google Murray Bookchin!

In recent years, a seemingly unlikely image has become popular in online leftist youth culture: that of the late twentieth-century philosopher Murray Bookchin (1921–2006). At first glance, Bookchin seems to be the opposite of what today's supposedly image-obsessed youth admire. Typically seen with glasses and a mustache, dressed in workday pants and suspenders, Bookchin epitomizes an ordinary man of the silent generation. Yet the new generation has portrayed this blue-collar persona in a humorous and, indeed, hopeful light. Memes encouraging people to "Google Murray Bookchin!" juxtapose his image with stereotypical items such as sunglasses, cigars, and exaggerated, muscular arms. He appears as cool and a cunning grandfather who almost dares the viewer into his utopian way of seeing the world.

That utopian outlook, called social ecology, was produced in the midst of tremendous intellectual, political-economic, and technological transformations at the intersection of nature and society. Over the course of six prolific decades, Bookchin elaborated social ecology in more than two dozen books, published well over a hundred articles, and gave countless speeches, talks, and lectures. Mobilizing history, ecology, social science, metaphysics, and political theory, he called to not only abolish capitalism but also dismantle the state and undo all systems of hierarchy and domination. Contemporary common sense dismisses the idea of abolishing hierarchy as absurdly impractical, even impossible. Yet Bookchin argued that that is precisely what we must do to survive as a species. As he is often quoted: "If we do not do the impossible, we shall be faced with the unthinkable."[1]

Scholars and activists widely regard Bookchin as one of the most groundbreaking thinkers of our time. Like most provocative thinkers, his legacy is fraught. Many readers find themselves daunted by his complex ideas and intricate writing style. His books routinely invoke sophisticated philosophical concepts, advanced vocabulary, and relatively obscure historical events that are unfamiliar to most readers without an advanced liberal arts education.

And, for all his many admirers, he has perhaps as many detractors who fiercely criticize him with labels such as grandiose and dogmatic or (with no small amount of ageism) grumpy and out of touch.

In *Recovering Bookchin*, political theorist Andy Price investigates what he calls the "Bookchin caricature," tracing its origins to polemical debates with fellow thinkers in the radical ecology and anarchist movements of the 1980s and 1990s. One unfortunate effect of the Bookchin caricature, Price argues, is that the originality and power of Bookchin's work has been lost. That is, people capitulate to the caricature without following up on the substance of those debates and discovering that Bookchin was often making valid points about humanism, mysticism, and right-wing ecology that are today widely regarded as true. Another unfortunate result of this divided literature is that it tends to get bogged down in the minutiae of what Bookchin did or didn't say. Devout reverence and excessive criticism for Bookchin as an individual *both* impede wider reflection on the social ecology movement.

This contribution to Pluto's FireWorks series reintroduces social ecology as both a set of ideas and a social movement. Without diminishing the importance of theoretical debate, I seek to bypass some of the roadblocks that impede Bookchin's most valuable insights from reaching a wide audience. To aid in this, I invoke the notion of *praxis*, the conscious integration of theory and action. Taking political action means attempting to realize one's ideals in real life. Yet, inevitably, real life does not conform to what we imagine. Praxis means taking unexpected outcomes – both the good and bad – as occasions to revise theory and, in turn, improve future democratic experiments. This book guides readers through a world where environmental philosophy meets democratic politics in a quest for deep system change. Drawing on years of ethnographic fieldwork and lived experience, it focuses on the messy and inventive processes through which activists invoke, challenge, reassess, and cross-pollinate social ecology's principles to invent and refine new democratic forms.

Chapter 1 sets the stage for this rich world of present-day activism and characterizes the stakes of the current historical moment. This moment demands deep transformations to our social fabric, not mere policy adjustments or more superficial forms of system change. Chapter 1 then briefly summarizes the historical background on the social ecology movement and introduces the Kurdish

Freedom Movement, one of the most exciting and celebrated examples of social-ecological activism today.

Another dilemma for the social ecology movement is that Bookchin's writing can be complicated and, for many, difficult to understand. Grappling with his work requires commitment and patience and, often, a robust background in philosophy, Marxian theory, sociology, and anthropology. Unfortunately, universities provide few opportunities to acquire this background. Bookchin himself was no academic – he earned the equivalent of a high school degree while studying electrical engineering at a technical institute but was otherwise educated in movement-aligned affinity groups and study circles.[2] More importantly, his revolutionary objectives often stood outside academic disciplinary concerns. In many ways, this freed Bookchin from the constraints of conventional academic scholarship that would otherwise have stifled his vision. On the other hand, it left his work without a disciplinary home where methodical study of his ideas could take place. The memes, graffiti, protest signs, buttons, and T-shirts cheekily urging people to "Google Murray Bookchin!" speak to this convoluted situation. For many, Google is, in fact, the most practical way to access his work.

Chapter 2 addresses this by sketching out the major contours of Bookchin's social ecology as a philosophy, focusing on four interrelated concepts: first and second nature, hierarchy, post-scarcity, and federal direct democracy. My aim is to provide a roadmap of social ecology's main arguments and commitments, giving students and non—academics the tools they need to understand the movements aligned with his ideas. To develop my perspective, I draw on many authors besides Bookchin, including social ecologists Dan Chodorkoff, Chaia Heller, and Modibo Kadalie, Kurdish thinkers Abdullah Öcalan and Dilar Dirik, as well as social theorists Judith Butler and David Graeber. Due to length constraints, I rarely give these authors more than passing attention. To address this, at the end of this book, I have provided a list of recommended readings with annotations to guide further inquiry. Wherever possible, I have attempted to use plain language and avoid jargon. Otherwise, I have provided a glossary to aid the reader. Despite these efforts, a brief conceptual outline cannot capture the full breadth or depth of Bookchin's ambitious work. For those looking for a more detailed scholarly analysis of Bookchin's work, I highly recommend Damian White's *Bookchin: A Critical Appraisal* and Andy Price's *Recovering Bookchin*.[3]

The remaining chapters pivot on how activists realize social-ecological principles in practice. Drawing on semi-structured interviews, primary and secondary historical research, and years of my own experience, I build case studies to show how egalitarian alternatives replace social hierarchies, foster symbiotic relationships between nature and humanity, and create bottom-up institutions of governance. These chapters are arranged by scale. Attitudes of domination seep into the deepest corners of our lives, shaping how we relate to ourselves and those closest to us. Chapter 3 therefore starts at the personal and interpersonal levels where activists foster personal and collective transformation. Often invoking the idea of "internal work," they develop introspective habits, egalitarian sensibilities, and collective actions such as affinity groups, self-criticism, and community-based justice. Chapter 4 turns to horizontal relationships that are open beyond immediate activist circles. Drawing on the anthropological work of Daniel Chodorkoff, I approach social ecology as a community-building effort that reweaves the everyday fabric uniting humans with our nonhuman neighbors. We will hear from ecovillage and permaculture practitioners involved in these struggles, paying special attention to how they have responded to dilemmas, contradictions, and critiques.

How might ecologically minded communities govern everyday life if given the opportunity? In Chapter 5, we delve into popular assemblies, the signature practice advocated by Bookchin and the social ecology movement. This chapter characterizes the key features and challenges of assemblies through the lens of movements such as Occupy Wall Street, Barcelona en Comú, and the Rojava Revolution. This chapter also looks at how Bookchin weighed in on these dilemmas, envisioning *libertarian municipalism* as a path to instituting popular, directly democratic governance. Chapter 6 continues this line of inquiry, examining federations as an ecologically informed alternative to the nation-state. Here, I draw on the case study of the Kurdish Freedom Movement and its program of democratic confederalism alongside the Zapatista Movement to illustrate why and how liberation movements are rejecting nationalism in favor of federal autonomy.

Pulling together these various case studies posed several conceptual challenges. Due to my personal background, language skills, and life experiences, the case studies in this book are predominantly in the Global North.

However, confederal politics and other social-ecological insights are largely rooted in the Global South, particularly among Indigenous communities. As an anthropologist, I am keenly aware that these communities have their own vocabularies and grammars of thought to describe their unique worldviews. Indigenous ways of thinking and being do not translate to any Western framework one-to-one. Indeed, many refuse the Western terms of "ecology" or "democracy" altogether. Nonetheless, I have used the terms "social ecologist" or "social-ecological" as a short-hand to indicate *a unity in diversity* where activists share a common vision-practice based around nonhierarchy, post-scarcity, and direct democracy. That being said, I do try to avoid too many liberties when applying the social ecology label.

At the same time, I have tried to capture an internal diversity within the self-described social ecology community. Social ecology is not the creation of a single person, springing fully formed from Murray Bookchin's mind like Athena from Zeus' forehead. It is a living tradition with multiple interpretations, applications, and intellectual histories. Indeed, there are many interpretations of social ecology, some of which have little to do with Bookchin at all (a topic discussed further later on). In the Kurdish Freedom Movement, the metaphor of a meadow is invoked to describe society: A "field with many flowers." I have kept this image at the forefront of my mind in portraying a movement of movements that is full of lively debate and disagreement.

Methodologically, this book blends activism and scholarship. In the summer of 2015, my department, the Department of Anthropology at the University of Massachusetts, Amherst, supported me in conducting ethnographic research and a master's thesis on climate justice movements in Catalonia and the Basque Country. Through my existing activist networks, that trip led me to North Kurdistan, where I had the privilege of meeting revolutionaries of the Kurdish Movement in the cities of Amed (Diyarbakir), Adana, and Urfa. As a doctoral student from 2017 to 2020, I followed up with university-approved research visits to Kurdish diaspora communities in Hamburg, Germany, and London, England. During this time, I also returned to Barcelona, a stronghold of the municipalist movement. While conducting this research, I helped organize protest campaigns, assemble newsletters, and publish press releases, and I followed the leadership of my activist peers and collaborators. Through these experiences, I conducted dozens of interviews, collected many pages of fieldwork notes, and participated in countless meetings and demonstrations. Quotes from these interviews and anecdotes from these experiences are peppered throughout the text. In compliance with my university's standing Institutional Review Board protocols, as well as in keeping with standard anthropological practice, I have referred to participants of this research who are not public figures or spokespersons via pseudonyms and stripped out other identifying information. Nevertheless, this book is not an ethnography in a strict sense. Like many radical scholars, I have juggled divergent commitments to activist and academic communities. Social movements often desire practical knowledge, while scholars produce knowledge based on ongoing debates. In this book, I have prioritized the activist calls for a fresh and accessible introduction to social ecology. Each chapter grapples with questions and dilemmas that emerge from activist critique, rather than from ongoing debates in anthropological research. Consequently, what I present here resembles a guidebook more than it does a classic "thick" ethnographic analysis.

The purpose of this book is to orient people outside of social ecology to its conversation about transformative change. Drawing together multiple voices, almost like a miniature assembly, it captures an ongoing dialog that will be of interest to a variety of audiences. For activists, this book provides a snapshot of the successes and challenges of the social ecology movement as well as food for thought about current dilemmas and areas for future growth. For educators, it offers a grounded account of how contemporary social movements link social and ecological transformation. Undergraduate-level readers should find its direct style clear and accessible.

My role in this dialog as the author is not to assert myself as an authority but to point out the connections between experiences. From Bookchin's home in Burlington, Vermont, to Rojava, Syria, a constellation of social movements points the way toward a new world. Fully realizing that world will take the creative contributions from many different kinds of people. By providing a glimpse of that constellation, I hope this book offers a sense of orientation and direction for those who today feel lost and overwhelmed by compounding crises.

CHAPTER ONE

Confronting the Polycrisis

Humanity is living through a period of profound crisis comprising many interlocking factors. Staggering material inequality, rising authoritarianism, tightening border regimes, climate change, pandemic disease, biodiversity loss and ecological collapse, war and global displacement, racialized violence, and mass incarceration are just some of the grave manifestations of that crisis. What we are up against is clearly more than a technical quandary or a period of temporary difficulty. For decades, we have observed cracks appear and spread between social and economic systems, political institutions, public infrastructure, goods and services, and ecological systems. Complexity theorist Edgar Morin names this pervasive and elusive pattern of dysfunction the polycrisis.[1] The notion is useful in foregrounding how a dispersed set of problems compound and reinforce one another. Capitalism, with its relentless exploitation of social and ecological systems, is a critical aspect of the polycrisis but it is not the only one. Hetero-patriarchy, colonization, and the state all contribute to this deeply fraught moment in world history.

Without a doubt, the crisis is psychological and relational just as much as it is practical or institutional. Societal dysfunction appears so widespread and complicated, it leaves us overwhelmed with a sense that little can be done. Dominant medicine treats addiction, depression, social isolation, and general malaise as individual problems, but the pervasiveness of these conditions speaks to a deeper collective anguish. Despair over the polycrisis also manifests in the proliferation of conspiracy theories and right-wing ideologies that scapegoat immigrants, women, LGBTQ+ people, and other minorities. Misanthropic fascination with war, overpopulation, and civilizational collapse saturate pop culture and seep into our imaginations. This atmosphere of hostility and division makes cooperation toward meaningful solutions even more difficult.

Like the Gordian knot of ancient Greek myth, this multifaceted crisis will only persist until the right instrument strikes through its core. Serious, self-conscious, and popular movements must forge liberatory institutions, systems, habits, and norms that cut through the old logics and categories. And these new modes of thinking and ways of life must free society from domination in all spheres of life. Where capitalism has tethered our material needs to the pursuit of profit, we must create sustainable economies that prioritize living systems and recognize ecological limits. Where patriarchy has denigrated feminized knowledge, values, and skills, we must demand men's full participation in household labor, reproductive care, and emotional development. In other words, people all over the Earth must collectively weave a new social fabric. This task is not a fantasy or an indulgence but an imperative for the survival of complex life on Earth. Already, climate change is causing sweeping planetary dislocations beyond anything our species has ever known.

Those seeking to confront the polycrisis encounter an oxymoron at the heart of so-called representative or parliamentary democracy. On the one hand, this currently prevailing political system is supposed to accommodate the will of everyday citizens. Rather than deciding on issues themselves, citizens entreat elected representatives who are supposed to vote in accordance with the desires and well-being of a majority of their constituents. On the other hand, in practice, this system rarely delivers meaningful participation. When ordinary people seek to direct public resources toward reconstructive projects and policies that actually benefit and improve communities, they find all too often that they cannot compete with corporations, landlords, businesses, and other moneyed interests. Public interest inherently contradicts the class interests of capitalists who want to sell people the means of life, but "representatives" are overwhelmingly drawn from this same moneyed class. Far from facilitating widespread civic participation, it usurps citizens' power to make decisions about their communities and transfers that power to professional bureaucrats.

Popular movements seeking change within the current system thus confront a paradox. To transform the capitalist system, we are told to elect friendly candidates to office and pursue gradual, limited reforms. And yet it seems that without capitalism limited democracy would collapse. Thus, to address deep-seated social problems, we must petition *the very same institutions responsible for those problems* in the first place. Black liberation activist and theorist Kali Akuno attributes this self-perpetuating cycle to what he calls the myth of democratic capitalism. Akuno, who is also a co-founder of the solidarity economy project Cooperation Jackson and the Racial and Environmental Justice Coordinator at the Institute for Social Ecology, writes that this false but convincing narrative positions democracy as "an almost inevitable byproduct of capitalism."[2] So long as movements only petition the current system, the cycle of dysfunction is self-perpetuating.

Reform under bourgeois capitalism can and does often improve living conditions, but this is inherently limited by deep contradictions at the core of our system of government. Truly addressing the global polycrisis means overcoming the myth of democratic capitalism and rejecting the false promises of representation under our current system. We need to institute new, genuinely participatory political institutions where *all* people can make meaningful decisions in the conditions of their everyday lives. Yet, in a turbulent and globalized world, this uncharted path leads to many questions. What kind of institutions are equipped to enable full and meaningful political participation? On what moral authority will those institutions stand? How will they juggle the imperative for local autonomy and self-determination with the reality of globalized supply chains, technologies, and communications? How will they relate to the economy? Can they ensure social justice? These are precisely the kinds of visionary questions that guide social-ecological activists as they square up to face the polycrisis.

WHAT IS SOCIAL ECOLOGY?

In the 1993 version of his cornerstone essay "What Is Social Ecology?," Bookchin defines social ecology as "the conviction that nearly all of our present ecological problems originate in deep-seated social problems."³ In light of present-day climate change, this observation may seem obvious. However, there is more to his carefully chosen words than meets the eye. By "deep-seated social problems," Bookchin asserts that nature and society cannot be separated while hinting at the problem of institutionalized domination. The possibility of a deeper transformation in the relationship between society and nature depends upon the dismantling of domination *in general*. That is, social hierarchy is a historical problem and is not naturally inevitable.

Much of Bookchin's extensive work explores the political implications of this central axiom. Advancing a holistic model of interaction between human and nonhuman worlds, he calls for a reevaluation of core beliefs about the human species. The prevailing capitalist model of society relates to the natural world primarily through exploitation. Social ecology contends that, despite these destructive tendencies, human intelligence and ingenuity can be marshaled as positive and life-affirming forces in natural evolution.

This book foregrounds social ecology as conceived by Bookchin. However, many thinkers have contributed to its development. Since the nineteenth century, socialist thinkers have recognized an impending collision between capitalism and nature. Prominent anarchists such as Peter Kropotkin and Élisée Reclus regarded humanity as having a meaningful role in the history of consciousness.⁴ Capitalism, as a system that is inherently exploitative of both nature and humans, disrupts our path of collective self-discovery. Karl Marx likewise recognized that nature and humans are integral, arguing that the contradictions of capitalist production inherently and inevitably alienate human beings from the nonhuman world – and, therefore, from ourselves.[5]

The term social ecology has been in use since the 1920s. Urban geographers have used social ecology as a kind of holistic inquiry into soil systems, hydrology, and other ecological phenomena that cross the boundaries of nature and society.[6] With the publication of *Community and Environment: A Discourse on Social Ecology* in 1953, the prolific city planner and architect Erwin Anton Gutkind pushed social ecology in a more radical direction. Making a passionate denunciation of the monotony and "massification" of consumerism, Gutkind likened cities to living organisms constituted by interdependent human and nonhuman inhabitants. Gutkind also saw nature and society as inextricably bound in a shared historical process. Like Bookchin, Gutkind believed in a society without capitalism or states and called for a utopian "revolution of the environment" that would radically decentralize modern cities into humanly scaled eco-communities.[7] According to Gutkind's contemporary, Peter Pfretzschner, Gutkind wrote in *Community and Environment*: "The emergence of communities in a stateless world is the highest ideal which we can discern at present."[8]

From its origins in urban studies, social ecology has been applied to a wide range of studies. In 1970, sociologist Arnold Binder established the Interdisciplinary School of Social Ecology at the University of California, Irvine to study the sociological impacts of interpersonal environments, societal conditions, and psychological states.[9] In 1983, Western Sydney University created a master's degree program in social ecology emphasizing participatory action research and learning as a transformational process.[10] Chaired for many years by Stuart Hill, the program approaches social ecology from an expansive perspective, embracing psychological, spiritual, and metaphysical inquiry, and teaches the development of ecological consciousness through active/empathic listening and deep leadership.[11] Recent publications from this area bring social-ecological analysis into the arts, drama, poetry, and religious studies.

Bookchin brought social ecology into the sphere of revolutionary philosophy. Born into a staunch leftist family during the 1920s, he came of age as the Soviet Union was clearly drifting into authoritarianism under Stalin. By the 1950s, industrial capitalism was also reaching its peak, with major advances in cybernetics and information technology rapidly appearing on the horizon. At the same time, a global ecological crisis was taking shape through issues such as soil erosion and chemical pollution. Ecology was a new and increasingly critical realm of thought. In this new science, Bookchin saw fertile ground to renew the philosophical foundations of revolutionary socialism. While we may think that ecology has little to do with political theory, there is a close relationship between how human beings treat each other and how we treat the natural world. Ideas about nature – in particular, *human* nature – shape our behavior, expectations, and beliefs about what kind of world is possible. In ecology, Bookchin found a worldview that prioritizes relationships over categories and open-endedness over scientific determinism. It was fertile ground for thinking through the deeper significance of a liberated society.

Still, it is one thing to theorize about a new social system and another to take responsibility for building that system. Bookchin was a committed, lifelong revolutionary who led a vibrant, fascinating life among intellectuals, organizers, bohemians, artists, feminists, Indigenous leaders, and other radicals.* His political life began in childhood, when he joined the Young Pioneers of America, a communist youth organization in the radicalized working-class neighborhood of Crotona Park in the Bronx, New York City. There, he served as a street orator selling copies of the organization's newspaper. As a young man during the 1950s, he joined the forward-thinking Marxist group Contemporary Issues, led by the former Trotskyist thinker Josef Weber, an experience discussed again in Chapter 2. The group was an incubator for his early intellectual work, in which he began to discuss an impending collision between capitalism and nature.

---

* Due to constraints of time and space, this book covers Bookchin's personal history only briefly. Readers interested in his biography can look to *Ecology or Catastrophe: The Life of Murray Bookchin*, authored by Bookchin's romantic partner and copyeditor, Janet Biehl. However, readers should be aware that, although the biography includes relevant biographical information, its standing and credibility among social ecologists is contested. In 2018, I co-authored a critical review in *Anarchist Studies* with Federico Venturini that addresses some of these problematic features, including a preponderance of speculative claims, as well as glaring omissions of important figures in Bookchin's personal and political life, including his children and former spouse, Beatrice. See Finley, E. and Venturini, F. (2018) "Ecology or Catastrophe: The Life of Murray Bookchin," *Anarchist Studies*, 26(1), 109–13, https://journals.lwbooks.co.uk/anarchiststudies/vol-25-issue-1/article-9320/.

During the 1960s, Bookchin joined the burgeoning anarchist movement in the Lower East Side and co-founded a new study-action group called Anarchos. He rose to fame with the famous pamphlet "Listen, Marxist!" urging Students for a Democratic Society, the flagship organization of the youth counterculture movement, to avoid a takeover by the Progressive Labor Party. This incisive critique led Bookchin to become a major figure of the budding radical ecology movement. He helped steer the Anti-Nuclear Movement of the 1970s and the Green Movement of the 1980s–1990s. He traveled extensively throughout Europe and North America and shared his views through numerous volumes, such as *The Ecology of Freedom: The Emergence and Dissolution of Hierarchy*, which many regard as his magnum opus.

During the latter half of his life, Bookchin settled in the city of Burlington, Vermont, a city with a living history of direct democracy. In Burlington, he and his inner circle experimented in stateless politics through civic and urban organization, launching the first chapter of the Green Movement in the United States, the Burlington Greens.

Generations of activists inspired by Bookchin have brought social-ecological thinking to radical movements throughout the US and beyond. In 1974, students from Goddard College, a small liberal arts college in central Vermont, set up an Institute for Social Ecology where Bookchin could teach while students gained firsthand experience in cutting-edge eco-technologies (Figures 1 and 2). Students from the institute went on to play key roles in organic agriculture and permaculture, ecological design, and solar and wind technologies. Institute students also went on to lead protest movements around climate and energy, genetically modified organisms (GMOs) and biotechnology, the Anti-Globalization Movement, and Occupy Wall Street. Chapter 3 looks at the community activism of the institute during its heyday. Those wanting to explore the history of the social movement further can look at works authored by institute educators themselves, including Brian Tokar's *The Green Alternative*, Dan Chodorkoff's *The Anthropology of Utopia*, and Chaia Heller's *The Ecology of Everyday Life*.

Figure 1   Bookchin teaching at the Institute for Social Ecology at Cate Farm

Source: Mark Ivins.

Today's social ecologists are active in many different spheres. In the economic sphere, they participate in worker and community cooperatives, participatory budgeting initiatives, mutual aid networks, and community resource libraries. Under the framework of a solidarity economy, these experiments provision goods and services in a just and sustainable way.[12] In the ecological sphere, social ecologists have led many initiatives such as those for permaculture food production, community-supported agriculture, ecological architecture and design, and urban "rewilding" projects. And of course, in the world of urban activism, they are active in promoting direct democracy and radical approaches to citizenship.

Figure 2   The Institute for Social Ecology at Cate Farm
Source: Mark Ivins.

THE ROJAVA REVOLUTION

Compelling ideas often travel to unexpected places. Leaders of the International Workingmen's Association of the late nineteenth century looked to industrialized countries such as Germany or England to spearhead a global socialist revolution. They scarcely imagined that Russia, a largely rural country with a still quasi-feudal political economy, would become the very first revolutionary Marxist nation via the Russian Revolution, starting in 1917.

Bookchin similarly oriented his ideas of libertarian municipalism and communalism to the cultural and political history of his home in the United States. Yet during the final years of his life, Bookchin's ideas were quietly taking root in another corner of the globe: the Kurdish-dominant regions of southeast Turkey and northeast Syria, respectively called "Bakur," meaning "North," and "Rojava," meaning "West," in the Kurmanji language. In 2012, the Rojava Revolution became the first major uprising to invoke Bookchin's vision, bringing confederal direct democracy to the center of global geopolitics and redefining "democratization" in the Middle East.

Journalists, international relations analysts, and other media commentators on Kurdish geopolitics repeatedly characterize this encounter between Bookchin's notion of confederal direct democracy and the Kurdish Freedom Movement as unlikely, "surprising," or "strange."[13] Yet a close inspection of the Kurdish Movement's history and concerns, including the deeper cultural history of Mesopotamia, reveals fascinating and compelling reasons why the movement for Kurdish liberation has arrived at this anti-nationalist paradigm.

The proximate story centers on the reorientation of the Kurdistan Workers' Party (PKK), spurred by the organization's imprisoned leader Abdullah Öcalan. Originating in national liberation movements of the 1970s, the PKK sought to establish an official, independent Kurdish state. For decades, they did so through the classic vanguard and guerrilla tactics and revolutionary worldview of Marxist Leninism and Maoism. By the mid-1990s, however, the group was clearly adopting different priorities, growing more focused on civil society initiatives, and cultivating revolutionary consciousness among the broader populace.

With the NATO-led abduction and imprisonment of Öcalan in 1999, he was appointed as a representative on behalf of the Kurdish people in negotiations with the Turkish government. At this point, Öcalan committed himself to designing a viable path forward that could stymie the bloodshed and deliver Kurdish autonomy. His intellectual engagement was profound, as he read as widely and broadly as possible, finding ingredients for this alternative model in leftist thinkers and scholars such as Michel Foucault, Immanuel Wallerstein, and Maria Mies. However, in Murray Bookchin's communalism, Öcalan discovered something unique: not only a critique of today's global capitalist system but also a positive proposal for a new political system or a "democracy without a state." Declaring Bookchin his teacher (*momosta*), a designation of the utmost respect in Kurdish culture, Öcalan articulated a philosophy of democratic confederalism alongside a concrete program of democratic autonomy for Kurdish-majority regions. As a nonstate political administration, the new paradigm is "flexible, multicultural, anti-monopolistic, and consensus-oriented,"[14] seeking coexistence alongside other political groups and factions. It was also a practical way of dealing with the reality of the Turkish state, the second most powerful military force in NATO.

Yet democratic confederalism has deeper significance for Kurds, the Middle East, and humanity in general. Kurds are one of the largest stateless ethnic minorities in the world. Since the dissolution of the Ottoman Empire, the four borders of Syria, Iraq, Iran, and Turkey have split their homeland. Nationalism in these countries has led to government policies of cultural erasure and genocide against Kurds. Kurdish repression is one of many ethno-nationalist conflicts in the Middle East tied to capitalist development, growing socio-economic inequality, and ecological degradation in noncapitalist parts of the world. Democratic confederalism promises a vision of Kurdish autonomy without reproducing the evils of nationalism and the state and inflicting them on minorities in a Kurdish nation-state. From conflict and repression, the Kurdish Freedom Movement aims to reclaim the historical agency of the people of the Middle East, valorizing its vast socio-cultural diversity and rich cultural heritage.

The outbreak of the Syrian Civil War in 2011–12 opened a vast new terrain in this struggle for multicultural, multiethnic autonomy. As the Baath Party lost control over Kurdish-majority regions in northern Syria, the PKK's sister party, the Democratic Union Party (PYD), asserted control over critical infrastructure. After nearly a decade of clandestine organizing, the movement established countless new civil entities, including schools, economic cooperatives, and citizen-led judicial committees, as well as a civil administration to coordinate them called the Movement for a Democratic Society (TEV-DEM). Guided by Öcalan's philosophy, TEV-DEM sent contingents from village to village, teaching and encouraging the people how to create communes and assemblies. To protect the fledging polity, citizen-led militias were called People's Protection Units (YPG) and Women's Protection Units (YPJ). Soon enough, these courageous forces were at war with the genocidal Islamic State, which had sought to destroy Kurds in Iraq and Syria once and for all.

Over the last 20 years, countless civil society projects have been created on both sides of the Turkish–Syrian border, including environmental and ecological initiatives, women's collectives and cooperatives, community-based justice, artists collectives, student unions, popular education projects, and village communes. In these projects, women are often the central protagonists. Indeed, women's liberation, ecological restoration, and cultural pluralism go hand in hand as activists restore the culture and ecology of the broader Middle East. Borrowing the language of Latin American political theorist Raúl Zibechi, we might regard Rojava as a *society in movement*.[15] A social movement rallies a marginal section of a given population toward specific goals or campaign objectives. Rojava, by contrast, involves all sectors of the population – old and young, men and women – in an open-ended and ongoing transformation. City by city, village by village, diverse cultures, religions, and social identities in southeast Turkey and northeast Syria experience liberatory activity on a daily basis.

Although Bookchin's philosophy has been a critical inspiration for the Rojava Revolution, it is erroneous to regard the Kurdish Movement as merely "implementing" his ideas. Those who implicitly regard the Rojava Revolution as solely a result of Bookchin's ideas perpetuate colonial intellectual power dynamics where implicitly marginalized groups are passive recipients of ideas generated in the Euro-American sphere. When we lose sight of this, we lose sight of the local conditions, sensibilities, and aspirations that made the revolution possible. Through the Rojava Revolution, there are now five million people living within democratic confederalism, with each individual making creative and courageous contributions despite tremendous repression and violence. It can only be understood in its own terms and through its own history.

In this way, the Rojava Revolution presents a new vantage point from which to view and even critique the social ecology tradition. What have Kurdish activists done differently and why? What have they found most useful in Bookchin's work? What would they wish or expect of their comrades in other parts of the world? The Rojava Revolution has stimulated numerous international forums, collaborative publications, and encounters, drawing social ecologists into conversation with activists from many global struggles, such as the Zapatistas, the Mapuche, or the Basque and Catalan independence struggles. In this dialog, a new international solidarity is possible through genuine pluralism and mutual understanding.

CONCLUSION

Social ecology is one facet of an emerging movement of movements. Although locally rooted and geographically dispersed, this movement of movements overlaps remarkably in terms of values, principles, and practices. As we shall see, the organizations and initiatives that appear in this book share deep commitments around social justice and antiracism, reproductive freedom, and bodily autonomy. Indigenous sovereignty and decolonization, the publicization of housing, healthcare, and other basic necessities, and community-based justice are also critical features. To achieve their aims, these movements are adopting assembly practices, autonomous federations, and decision-making practices over the prevailing convention of centralized leadership and parties.

This is not to say that all reconstructive movements think and act the same way. On the contrary, plurality is another key feature of the emerging paradigm. Instead of a singular "movement" committed to the same strategies, we see a diversity of movements committed to life-affirming values. Indigenous movements play a major role in maintaining and defending this plurality. Indigenous societies around the world have fundamentally different conceptions of things such as nature, culture, time, or what it means to have agency or to be alive. Anthropologists such as Marisol de la Cadena and Arturo Escobar call this "ontological pluralism."[16] The Zapatista Movement in Chiapas (Mexico) captures the spirit of ontological pluralism with its famous defense of "one world where many worlds fit." That is, we can see and do things differently while sharing a life-affirming worldview. Bookchin arrives at a similar notion in conceptual vocabulary with the principle of *unity in diversity*. In natural ecology, diversity is a fundamental marker of health in an ecosystem. Diversity – both in social worlds and ecological contexts – is a strength that corresponds to greater overall stability in that system.

Unity in diversity will be a critical principle for solving the polycrisis. Capitalism and hierarchical society have made our world monotonous, predictable, and therefore controllable. Today's movements must reclaim the individual character of communities, saving precious human and ecological systems and asserting humanity's potential as a positive force on this planet. We are entering a period of profound crises. But we have what we need to face those crises if we know where to look. Social movements are developing the technological, economic, social, and conceptual tools necessary to confront catastrophe and demand utopia.

CHAPTER TWO

The Theory of Social Ecology

In August of 2011, when I was in my early twenties, I found myself in the peaceful and idyllic countryside of central Vermont. Gathered in a refurbished barn-turned-meeting space with friends and members of the Institute for Social Ecology, I had my first up-close look at social ecology's directly democratic vision of the world. Little did I know, in just a few short weeks, that vision would erupt into town squares, plazas, and parks across the country through the Occupy Wall Street Movement. From 2010 to 2013, similar mobilizations sent shock waves through Latin America, Europe, the Middle East, and North Africa as ordinary people collectively raised their voices against neoliberal austerity. At the same time, although it was not reported in the media, revolutionaries in North Kurdistan were also creating a new way of life built around assemblies. Soon I, too, became immersed in the call for real democracy.

The theory of social ecology has provided a touchstone for activists for more than 50 years. The folks I met that summer at the institute have also been key figures in movements ranging from the Anti-Nuclear Movement to Occupy Wall Street. Year after year, these diverse and remarkable people come together from remote corners of the world because of their commitment to a common revolutionary outlook. This chapter breaks that outlook down into four interrelated concepts:

- first and second nature,
- nonhierarchy,
- post-scarcity, and
- direct democracy.

I have taken this analytic approach in the hope of offering a relatively simple introduction that readers without a background in advanced theory can follow. Nonetheless, it is important to remember that social ecology is a dialectical philosophy, meaning its significance can only be fully conveyed by modeling how its various concepts are integrated. For a more comprehensive introduction to social ecology, I recommend Bookchin's compelling and succinct book *Remaking Society*, originally published in 1989. More seasoned readers will no doubt notice that I have also omitted many important ideas from Bookchin's conceptual vocabulary, such as his radical redefinitions of citizenship, politics, and the city. Due to time and length restrictions, what follows here is a sketch of social ecology's main concepts. Still, I hope some of those additional concepts will also become clearer along the way.

FIRST AND SECOND NATURE

Social ecology is grounded in the attempt to undo the erroneous dualism between society and nature that underpins much of Western cosmology. According to this view, society and nature are effectively separate realms, each governed by different laws and logics. Under many circumstances, dualistic thinking can be helpful. Without it, we would not have fields such as computer science, engineering, mathematics, physics, or analytic philosophy. However, dualistic thinking cannot really explain the fluid and continuous activity of organic life. Consider, for example, the growth of a tree. Individual branches sprout from a central trunk in a continuous way, without "sudden jumps or entrances."[1] At a certain, yet indefinable, point the branch and trunk cohere, which in turn transitions seamlessly to the root system. Dualism oversimplifies this complex reality. Indeed, dualistic thinking in life oversimplifies many everyday realities, such as gender and sexual identity or ethnic and cultural identities. Life is characterized by gradients, contradictions, and differentiation.

The current ecological crisis has forced even the most intransigent people to recognize that nature and society are deeply connected. However, the temptation to reproduce binary thinking is persistent, leading many well-meaning people to exalt nature while maligning society. In *The Ecology of Everyday Life*, feminist social ecologist and anthropologist Chaia Heller deconstructs dualistic ideology around nature and gender, showing that romantic idealization is just another form of alienation and degradation.[2] What matters is not so much *that* nature and society are integrated but rather *how*. Human society is derived from nonhuman nature somewhat like a branch of a tree. Society is distinct from nature yet cannot be uprooted from it.

Crucially, social ecology conceives nonhuman nature as a *historical process*. This process began some four billion years ago, with the advent of organic life in clouds of simple bacteria. Even these ancient life forms showed a certain degree of self-organization and self-realization as they gravitated toward food or avoided environmental toxins. The earliest animals didn't scuttle along the murky ocean seafloor until some 2.5 billion years later and it wasn't until the "Cambrian explosion" approximately 542 million years ago that we begin to see the "basic animal forms."[3] Over this unfathomably long arc, the diversity of organic life accumulated. As new organisms emerge, so too do a wide array of relational ecosystems, niches, and communities. This organic diversity promotes stability, in turn enabling more nuanced relationships between organisms and their environment. As evolution creates new and more complex forms of consciousness, animals begin to do more than adapt to their environment; rather, they change their environment itself.

Another feature of natural evolution or "first nature" is the tendency toward greater degrees of sociality and interaction. For hundreds of millions of years, our planet's organisms barely interacted with one another. In the Cambrian explosion, we finally see specialized appendages such as antennae, fins, eyes, and teeth. With the rise of Darwin's theory of natural selection at the end of the nineteenth century, anarchist philosopher Peter Kropotkin argued that cooperation, not competition, was the dominant factor in evolution.[4] Drawing on scientific observations of a wide range of creatures, including flocks of birds, schools of fish, herds of bison, bands of apes, and other animals, he argued that organisms become more cooperative as they become more evolved and complex. The emergence of mammals some 40 million years ago is especially significant. Mammals are distinguished by a prolonged period of close proximity between parents and offspring. Entire extended family groups thus become responsible for the group's care. And through these sustained relationships, mammals impute learned behavior to their infants. Learned behavior replaces instinct. And cooperation makes that possible.

The arrival of *Homo sapiens* brings natural evolution to a new threshold. Humans have the capacity to alter our physical environment to a qualitatively new level. From fashioning stone tools and lighting campfires to constructing dwellings, clothing our bodies, and domesticating animals, we seem to create an artificial world. The human capacity for language and culture allows us to maintain these skills, knowledge, and traditions within institutions. Bookchin, drawing from the tradition of Aristotle, call this new branch of evolution "second nature." Second nature exists within our own minds just as much as it does in material reality. It includes our technical skills, daily habits, sense of humor, language skills, and artistic traditions.

Finally, through humans, nature is conscious and aware of itself. The human brain itself retells this story as our "reptilian" hind brain houses basic motor functions, while the mammalian center gives rise to our emotions, and the frontal cortex houses reason, problem-solving, and awareness of time and consequences. The quest for freedom, ethics, and justice that direct democracy embodies is itself rooted in biology because *we* are rooted in biology.

Indigenous communities have long recognized human beings' role in nature *as* nature. Their practices model sustainable relationships to land, reflecting a broader outlook of responsibility toward nonhuman nature.[5] The seriousness of that responsibility is evident in the fact that Indigenous communities inhabit 20 percent of the Earth's land yet protect up to 80 percent of the planet's biodiversity.[6] Article 1 of the "Universal Declaration of the Rights of Mother Earth" sets the stage for the legal recognition of humanity's moral responsibility to nature in the international community. Issued in Cochabamba, Bolivia, at the World People's Conference on Earth Day, 2010, the declaration asserts that human rights – especially Indigenous rights – extend to the nonhuman nature of which we are a part: "We, the peoples and nations of Earth ... are all part of Mother Earth, an indivisible, living community of interrelated and interdependent beings with a common destiny."

Radical movements in the West are also advancing the idea of conscious nature. Before Bookchin, the anarchist geologist Elisée Reclus wrote that human beings are "nature becoming conscious of itself."[7] Recent work by Marxian scholars such as Kohei Saito, who closely examined Marx's journals, shows that Marx shared these views to a great extent and understood the impending collision between capitalism and the environment.[8]

Bookchin believed that conscious nature presents the possibility of a new evolutionary stage: a "third nature" where human beings apply our creative capacities to foster nonhuman consciousness. If all human experience once laid dormant within clouds of ancient bacteria, so too there are vast potentialities of consciousness hidden within the present moment. It is supremely ironic that today's capitalist society has put technologists on the fool's errand of pulling "artificial intelligence" out of inert plastics and metals when the nonhuman intelligences of animals, plants, fungi, and bacteria are *right in front of us*. Even worse, the absurdly intensive energy consumption of AI data centers only drives those precious intelligences further into oblivion. Nonetheless, third nature remains an inherent potentiality within humanity's collective grasp, even if today it seems like a distant science fiction fantasy.

NONHIERARCHY

If human beings have such a special place in natural evolution, why has second nature already had such a devastating impact on first nature? In just a few short centuries, urban sprawl, monoculture, agriculture, mining, and industry have obliterated global ecosystems that took millions of years to develop. According to the International Union for the Conservation of Nature, up to 150 plant and animal species become extinct every single day, and even this number is likely to be significantly underreported.[9] Just as alarmingly, recent studies show that the total amount of global human-made material on the planet now surpasses organic mass.[10] Clearly, something has gone terribly wrong.

Data show that a small population of wealthy elites has created, enabled, and profited from ecological exploitation and collapse. Since 1988, just 100 companies have caused more than 70 percent of the world's greenhouse gas emissions.[11] Private jets of the ultra-wealthy alone produce approximately 1.25 percent of total global carbon emissions. This top 1 percent represents half of all the world's aviation emissions. Recently, it came to light that

Exxon and other oil giants made accurate predictions about climate change *as early as the 1950s*. Not only did Exxon bury these data, but they actively thwarted efforts to avert the impending catastrophe via lobbying and legislation. "The Earth is not dying," the folk singer and labor organizer Utah Phillips is supposed to have said, "It is being killed, and those who are killing it have names and addresses." Now, the same industries that created it in the first place are claiming to offer technical solutions.

But relentless resource extraction is not produced by the greed or selfishness of individuals; it is the inevitable result of an economic system based on endless growth. As an economy defined by endless production and accumulation, capitalism is inherently incapable of heeding the limits of our planet's biosphere. In the marketplace, Bookchin observes, "sheer survival requires that the entrepreneur expand his or her productive apparatus in order to remain ahead of others." Without growth, a company falls prey to its competitors. In this way, the only option for a company is to expand. "The key to this law of life – to survival – is the expansion and the quest for ever-greater profits, to be invested, in turn, in still further expansion."[12] And when we are all compelled to participate in companies to feed our families, that system can continue indefinitely.

If capitalism has inevitably led us to the ecological crisis, then we might reasonably ask what has led us to capitalism. Karl Marx keenly emphasizes that capitalism is not only an economic system or a way of managing resources and material goods. We too are arranged by the market. Instead of collaborating with friends, family, and neighbors, we become self-interested buyers, sellers, and wage laborers. At its heart, capitalism is a social system that organizes people and relationships. And the relationships that capitalism produces are *hierarchical*. Hierarchy is a term from the field of anthropology; it refers to social systems and institutions that use coercion to divide people into superior and inferior groups. Hierarchies can be informal, such as in the subordination of women in the household, or highly formalized, such as in the prison system.

One of the defining arguments of Bookchin's career was the idea that any attempt to abolish capitalism in particular without abolishing hierarchy in general would only recreate the conditions that created capitalism to begin with. The Old Left had failed to address the hierarchical institution of the state and thus devolved into bureaucratic authoritarianism. Any contemporary movement against capitalism that fails to consistently address hierarchy and the state is doomed to repeat that fatal error.

States create the social and political conditions for capitalism. States are defined by a hierarchy of violence via police, standing armies, chronic warfare, and imperial expansion. They must constantly struggle over territory, maneuvering to maintain control over borders and fend off rivals. The violence of the state also extends internally as aristocrats and other high-status individuals must keep a firm grip on their subordinates. The purpose of the police is to control these underclasses, who pose the constant threat of rebellion. Without this systemic violence and coercion, capitalist economies would collapse.

States are also ecologically devastating by themselves. At the peak of European colonialism, vast swathes of

Europe were deforested to construct its armadas. Today, the single greatest institutional producer of greenhouse gases is the United States Department of Defense. According to researchers at the Watson Institute of Public Affairs, since the beginning of the War on Terror in 2001, the US military has emitted 1.2 billion metric tons of greenhouse gases. Annually, that's equivalent to more than 250 million passenger cars, twice the number of cars currently on the road in the US.[13]

Yet states themselves are constructed upon patriarchy, ageism, and other forms of domination. In her incisive critique of anthropological theory, *Making Gender*, Sherry Ortner demonstrates how the subjugation of women is a product of state development, arguing that women are only subjugated for their reproductive capacities once there is a social ladder to climb.[14] State hierarchies depend upon aristocracies predicated on lineage and descent. In such systems, marriage is a primary means of social mobility. Families restrict and control their daughters' movements as the social status of the entire family depends upon her ostensible sexual "purity."

Bookchin saw hierarchy as a historical development, not a natural inevitability. In fact, he saw human history as broken into two primary streams: a history of hierarchical society and a history of freedom. According to Bookchin, the history of freedom originates from "organic society," which encompasses prehistoric modes of social organization based on interdependence, respect for individuals, and group solidarity. In his seminal work, *The Ecology of Freedom*, he traces the dialog of freedom and unfreedom from the emergence of hierarchy through the rebellions in the Middle Ages to the establishment of universal, humanist principles and the modern anarchist movement.

Today's prevailing cultural narrative holds that social hierarchy is necessary for social complexity. We may dislike social class and state rule, but they are necessary evils because egalitarian societies are simple and small and lack the comforts of civilization. This grand civilizational narrative pervades modern academia; however, many of its central assumptions are false. In *The Dawn of Everything*, David Graeber and David Wengrow synthesize the abundance of recent research in anthropology, archaeology, paleoarchaeology, and paleogenetics, showing that prehistoric societies were not limited to small and equalitarian bands. These studies show that many people lived in complex, decentralized social configurations. Many early cities were organized on complex, egalitarian lines, without rulers or administrators. The long period of human prehistory resembled, according to Graeber and Wengrow, a "carnival parade of political forms and social experiments."[15]

We do not need to appeal to ancient times in order to see that complex societies can be organized nonhierarchically. Every egalitarian and mutualistic relationship we have testifies that dominance and submission are not immutable or inevitable. In *The Modern Crises*, Bookchin astutely observes that the fact that hierarchy often seems inevitable is just another product of living within a hierarchy. The ideology of our time projects hierarchy onto nonhuman nature, seeing domination where instead there is interdependence: "Lions are turned into 'kings of beasts' only by human kings," he writes, "and ants belong to the 'lowly' only by virtue of ideologies spawned in temples, palaces, and manors."[16] The next two sections consider what social ecologists think life could look like without palaces and manors.

POST-SCARCITY

The material conditions of an egalitarian society do not have to be meager or harsh. In fact, recent advances in fields such as telecommunications, nanotechnologies, computation, manufacturing, and agricultural science have reached a point where toil and deprivation could be unnecessary. Bookchin argued as early as the mid-1960s – as the digital technologies of the so-called Third Industrial Revolution were just coming into view – that advanced technologies could pave the way for a "post-scarcity society" in which they would be applied in ethical, ecological, and democratic ways. If the struggle for food and shelter once compelled hierarchies during previous eras of human history, that struggle was now obsolete. In 1967, he surmised: "Bourgeois society, if it achieved nothing else, revolutionized the means of production on a scale unprecedented in history."[17] Without the pressure of survival, people could focus on desirable activities such as art and creative pursuits, leisure, social events, and time in nature. Individuals could reach their true potential by pursuing their passions and talents.

Needless to say, the vast majority of people never see the potential benefits of technology. On the contrary, our present technology often produces scarcity in the service of capital as the world's poor endure grueling working conditions within factories, mines, and industrial plants to produce cables, computer chips, batteries, and other technology parts. Even for the middle classes who can afford access to consumer goods, technology does not reduce the burdens of wage labor, debt, rent, and mortgages. In recent years, corporate executives have promised that advanced algorithmic technologies or AI will lessen workloads, but in practice they invoke the expense of these technologies to justify laying off their workers.[18]

A post-scarcity society would redirect technological power in socially liberating and ecologically sustainable ways. Communities in a post-scarcity economy would produce locally to meet their own needs for food, energy, transportation, and social services. That production would be attuned to local environmental needs and characteristics. Decisions about energy production, for instance, would account for that region's ecological profile. If the region has an abundance of rivers and streams, then a community will adopt a primarily hydropower energy profile as opposed to solar or wind.

By definition, this form of economy would be democratic. Decisions over major features of the economy, such as what and how much to produce, would be made by the community as a whole. Neighborhood workshops could provide tool libraries, training and workshops, and other resources necessary for technical tasks, such as carpentry and automotive mechanics. Even industrial manufacturing could be pursued on a local scale. Neighborhood workshops could house multipurpose machines where many of the heavy materials needed for construction and infrastructure could be produced. During Bookchin's lifetime, such community-based production was largely a matter of imagination. Today, however, many communities already possess some of these productive capacities in the form of community production centers, public 3D printers, tool libraries, and maker spaces.

Even though a post-scarcity society would make use of many modern technologies, luxury and wealth would look very different to today. Under capitalism, wealth is defined by material possessions such as houses and cars, electronics and computer games, gadgets and toys, fast fashion, and cosmetics. These objects represent a deeply distorted sense of well-being in which accumulation and acquisition are substitutes for genuinely meaningful self-expression and participation within communities. Moreover, the unsustainable and exploitative nature of their production is also largely concealed from consumers. A post-scarcity society would seek new ethical forms of comfort and affluence, such as public arts, welcoming public spaces, and community activities and events. Individuals in a post-scarcity society would also focus on restoring ordinary pleasures, nutritious food, regular physical exercise, sufficient sleep, time with friends and family, rest and leisure, and access to the outdoors.

Many of the features of a post-scarcity society align with the call for degrowth. Degrowth refers to the controlled downscaling of global material and energetic consumption.[19] Emerging from the field of ecological economics, degrowth scholarship demonstrates that our society's current patterns of consumption utterly outpace our planet's capacity to renew those resources. We have already crossed numerous planetary boundaries or tipping points that will permanently destabilize the Earth's critical systems. Stabilizing global production and consumption is an urgent matter that demands sweeping changes to our day-to-day lives. Degrowth scholarship therefore also looks at how to eliminate dependence on fossil fuels, localize global supply chains, and vastly reduce material waste, among other important measures. In calling for the communalization or municipalization of luxury, post-scarcity exposes that a great deal of society's consumer waste is preventable. The need for individual "conveniences," such as single-use plastics and individual-occupancy vehicles, could be made obsolete by collective conveniences such as clean waterways and abundant public transportation.

Post-scarcity would see a collective shift from a mentality of acquisition toward a mentality of abundance. Once again, Indigenous traditions offer some guidance on how to cultivate that collective perspective. For example, according to the Great Law of Peace of the Great Lakes region in North America, Six Nations peoples recite a covenant with nature called the Thanksgiving Address. Before every gathering, such as community assemblies, celebrations, and decision-making processes,[20] the assembled community gives thanks for every part of Creation, including animals, plants, and the elements. In one voice, the community celebrates each entity for fulfilling its "Creator-given duty" and supporting human life. In an interview with New York-based Potawatomi biologist Robin Wall Kimmerer, an Onondaga Nation clan mother reflects that the address "reminds you every day that you have enough – more than enough. Everything needed to sustain life is already here. When we do this, every day, it leads us to an outlook of contentment and respect for all of Creation."[21] Today, capitalism manufactures the illusion of scarcity by fostering dissatisfaction and discontent. Even radical Western thinkers such as Bookchin or Marx tend to promote technological advancement to solve natural scarcity. Yet, by stressing gratitude and responsibility, Indigenous ecologies challenge the assumption that our planet was ever naturally scarce to begin with.

DIRECT DEMOCRACY

Perhaps the defining feature of Bookchin's social ecology is its deep integration with political philosophy. In direct democracy, he found a political system that directly empowers ordinary people, embodying the ecological principles of diversity, creativity, and interdependence.

Direct democracy brings politics back into the realm of everyday life. It involves members of a community convening in face-to-face assemblies to debate and decide on issues that affect the community as a whole. These assemblies are held in public, easily accessible locations such as town halls, neighborhood councils, recreation centers, public schools, or libraries, and their time and location are publicized well in advance.

There are many misconceptions about direct democracy and how it could function today. One common misconception is that assemblies dictate the individual lives of their members. But this is not the case. In a liberatory society, assemblies are concerned with the public institutions that make community life possible, such as schools, hospitals, roads, farms, libraries, workshops, and other services. Individual liberty and personal initiative are valued as an aspect of the collective. Together, the individual members of a community create a unity in diversity.

Another misconception is that all members would have to make all decisions all the time. This also isn't precisely true. Experts such as scientists and technicians can be empowered to make designs and offer counsel in their area of specialization. For example, a team of civil engineers would be empowered to design the construction, operation, and maintenance of a bridge, but the decision whether or not to build the bridge would lie with the community as a whole.

Direct democracy recovers the humanity of politics. Under patriarchal capitalism, politics is conceptually divorced from and elevated above the personal. In political life, we are expected to be disembodied, rational, and objective (and of course, any claims that disrupt the prevailing power structure are dismissed as irrational and self-interested). But this claim to objectivity is a fantasy. In reality, each of us lives in a vulnerable human body; we have individual passions, proclivities, and special concerns. In her book *Toward a Performative Theory of Assembly*, social theorist Judith Butler writes that assembly politics are born from the inherent fact that "everyone is dependent on social relations and enduring infrastructure in order to maintain a livable life."[22] She defines assembly as "a collective artistry" that embraces subjectivity, individuality, and compromise.[23] By appearing together in person to decide the collective conditions of our lives, we acknowledge and confront our mutual vulnerability and interdependence.

Direct democracy embodies ecological principles. No two communities practice assemblies in the same way, illustrating the principle of diversity. Each community brings its own cultural values, preferences, and history. Likewise, the character of a session depends greatly upon who is present and on what terms. Real-life assemblies are constituted by living people with all of their flaws, prejudices, and idiosyncrasies. In this very human way of doing politics, leadership is not about implementing impartial rules but about cultivating trustworthiness.

Directly democratic assemblies put ecological decisions in the hands of the people who will confront their consequences. No rich man has ever set up a fracking rig in his own backyard. Environmental injustice is often a simple matter of powerful nation-states and corporations imposing the damaging impact of their activities on marginalized communities. For years, environmental justice research in the US has demonstrated that race is the most accurate single predictor of where toxic facilities are located.[24] Although there is no guarantee that democratically organized communities couldn't also make short-sighted environmental choices, they are disincentivized from polluting, exploiting, and degrading the biosystems upon which they depend. Communities are even less likely to exploit their surrounding ecosystems in a noncapitalist society where people are freed from the burden of wage labor. Indeed, it makes more sense to enhance ecosystems for the benefit of future generations. This logic is enshrined in the Haudenosaunee Seventh Generation Principle, which requires that all community decisions safeguard the well-being of descendants seven generations in the future.

When people join together to think and argue, a qualitatively different form of reason emerges. There is a shared agency or *intersubjectivity* through which citizens, neighbors, and fellow community members who share the same physical and social environment produce collective knowledge and understanding. The visionary anarchist Pierre-Joseph Proudhon calls this "collective reason," a cognitive form or "collective force."[25] Collective reason surpasses the scope and capacities of what those individuals can achieve individually. The hallmark of organic development is a striving toward greater consciousness and self-actualization. Collective reason expresses that tendency on another level, opening a new horizon for subjectivity, consciousness, and ethics.

The historical roots of assembly politics are deep. Evidence for assemblies dates back at least as far as Neolithic times. Indigenous peoples, peasant communities, and resistance movements worldwide have practiced them for time immemorial. For many communities, assemblies are important sites for communal identity. Assembly gatherings are often cultural events that accompany music, dancing, feasting or potlucks, singing, or spiritual ceremonies.

Skeptics often object that this form of governance is impractical for large groups of people and cannot be scaled up. Confederations, which are the subject of Chapter 6, address this limitation by convening spokespersons or *delegates* from each assembly. Delegates communicate the decisions made at the assembly level. But unlike representatives, their role is administrative not authoritative. As

Bookchin writes in *The Next Revolution*, "a confederalist view involves a clear distinction between policy-making and the coordination and execution of adopted policies."[26] Delegates embody the web of relationships between communities and help facilitate initiatives at the confederal level. If they stray too far in these duties, they can be easily recalled and replaced. Through delegates, communities can coordinate across many levels of scale, up to and including globally.

Direct democracy is a new form of political thinking about how power moves from the bottom up. While Bookchin has been an important catalyst for this thinking, his voice is just one within a rich and lively conversation. The Pan-African scholar Modibo Kadalie, for example, argues in his book *Pan-African Social Ecology* that face-to-face interactions, daily conversations, and everyday interconnection are central to making direct democracy work in the real world.[27] Kadalie contends that "intimate" direct democracy interwoven with eco-technologies and nonhierarchy is vital to the character of Indigenous African politics.[28] Historically, throughout the Great Dismal Swamp, maroon communities composed of self-liberated Black and Indigenous peoples practiced direct democracy. The legacies of these politics can be found in the intimate, everyday forms of resistance in Black communities. Kadalie's notion of intimate direct democracy is a warning against the temptation to get bogged down in hypothetical discussions about procedural details. While rules and guidelines are important, at the end of the day, direct democracy is not a set of procedures; it is a *process*. Real democracy is constituted in how we treat each other.

Theory shapes reality by guiding how people see and interact with the world. So far, this book has characterized social ecology as a radical worldview and the context of its formation. From here, we turn to how activists try to bring those ideals to life through practice. In their experiments, new questions, challenges, and opportunities come to the foreground, raising new possibilities for transformative change.

CHAPTER THREE

Laying the Groundwork

Newcomers to social ecology often think that its practice begins with organizing popular assemblies. After all, confederal direct democracy is the movement's signature idea. However, in my own years of experience, I have learned it is one thing to advocate for and even participate in direct democracy and quite another to be mentally and emotionally prepared for it. Direct democracy demands the ability to weigh our own needs and viewpoints alongside the needs and viewpoints of others. It requires active listening, persuasive public speaking, and emotional regulation, as well as consistency and follow-through – skills that take time and patience to learn.

In the course of writing this book, I formally interviewed or informally chatted with dozens of individuals from democratic projects, from internationally celebrated initiatives such as Barcelona en Comú in Spain and the PYD to relatively smaller projects such as Coalizione Civica in Bologna, Italy, or Portland Assembly in the US. Time and again, representatives emphasized the need for mental, emotional, and intellectual groundwork. Many shared stories of promising efforts that ended prematurely because the people spearheading them lacked strong relationships or conflict resolution skills. Reflecting on her own experience in a discontinued assembly project, Olivia, an activist based in the Pacific Northwest, calls for a better understanding within the movement of how hierarchical dynamics play out: "I think there is a feeling that reading Bookchin alone is enough to begin intensive movement-building projects ... But I don't think he knew (nor do many white men [know]) enough about interpersonal power dynamics and I see a really flattening out of these issues as all 'hierarchy.' It's more dynamic than that." Just as hierarchical society has eroded our ecological surroundings, it has also eroded our social and emotional capacities. Even the best democratic procedure cannot make up for the dysfunctional habits we learn while living under capitalism.

It is not only leaders who need to do the internal work. Kali Akuno, whose group Cooperation Jackson is a flagship of the solidarity economy movement, adds that dealing with hierarchical attitudes and habits is all the more challenging when working in the general population: "If you want to do mass work, you're going to have to deal with people who don't share your worldview. And if ideological purity is the measure of who you work with, you're going to be alone."

Committed revolutionary groups spend years laying the immaterial groundwork for their core members and base. Akuno notes that Cooperation Jackson, launched in Jackson, Mississippi in 2014, built upon popular militancy and strategic efforts from its founding members dating back to the early 1990s, efforts which themselves stemmed from the Black Power and Civil Rights Movements. Likewise, the Kurdish-led PYD trained underground for years in revolutionary theory and praxis before their historic opportunity arose in 2011–12. Even once the war had broken out, groups still focused on long-range planning, running limited experiments, and building revolutionary character. In the words of Mehmut Botan, a media specialist in the Kobanî Canton: "Revolution doesn't fall from the sky. It is the result of the accumulation of knowledge; the accumulation of organizing, of experience, and of struggle."

This chapter centers on the everyday solidarities, educational processes, and individual and collective emotional labor that constitute that "internal work." Although these practices receive relatively less attention than highly visible assemblies or protests, there is a growing literature among scholar-activists prioritizing the crucial link between mental and affective health and social transformation, including inspiring publications such as *Emergent Strategy* by adrienne marie browne, *Mutual Aid* by Dean Spade, and *Joyful Militancy* by carla bergman and Nick Montgomery. From study groups to self-criticism, activists are cultivating a resilient and insightful democratic culture.

EMOTIONAL HEALING

By the phrase "internal work," activists are often alluding to emotional healing and confrontation with personal suffering and turmoil. Personal healing comes in many different forms – from Western therapeutic techniques such as cognitive behavior therapy to meditative disciplines such as engaged Buddhism or somatic therapy. Bookchin famously opposed the individualistic and commercial aspects of these techniques. During his later years, he witnessed the rebellious hippie counterculture in the

1960s that he once found so promising absorbed into individualistic and commercial endeavors such as yoga, meditation, psychotherapy, and self-identified "Eastern" philosophy. He saw pop spiritualism and deep ecology as feeding into a destructive pattern of anti-rationalism, incoherence, or selfish individualism.

Years later, as society is undeniably in the midst of a full-blown global mental health crisis, many social ecology activists are trying to strike a middle ground. It has become clear the same hierarchical worldview that separates society and nature likewise separates body and mind. If we are serious about overcoming the objectification of nature, we must find ways to overcome the psychic and emotional objectification of the self. Skills such as mindfulness, emotional regulation, and compassionate curiosity are indispensable foundations of a democratic future.

Emotional healing does not have to come through individualistic or commercial endeavors. In social movements, relational models of self- and community-care are replacing conventional individualistic models of dealing with mental wellness. Health cooperatives, healing circles, and peer counseling networks demonstrate profound courage and speak to the widespread hunger for human connection. Indeed, some of the most powerful forms of healing come through human relationships.

The power of relationships was expressed in a particularly poignant way by a movement elder, Roberto Mendoza. Based in Tulsa, Oklahoma, Roberto is of Muscovy and Mexican-Indigenous heritage. He joined historic mobilizations of the American Indian and Chicano Liberation of the 1970s and, as a participant in the Green Movement in the 1980s, Mendoza discovered the practice of co-counseling. In this mutual therapeutic technique, participants break into turn-taking pairs to confront past hurts and adverse experiences. While one co-counselor reflects on those hurts, the other engages in nonjudgmental, active listening. By fostering healing through mutual empathy and reciprocity, co-counseling attempts to break conventional therapy's top-down dynamic between practitioner and patient.

These days, Roberto dedicates his energy to giving workshops on the similarities between social ecology and Indigenous ethical values of cooperation, reciprocity, horizontality, local autonomy, food sovereignty, and Earth-centered spirituality. It is around this topic that he and I developed a correspondence. One evening, as a particularly long interview was drawing to a close, I confided to Roberto that I had recently been feeling lonely and disconnected, thanking him sincerely for our dialog. For a moment, there was a pause, and then Roberto replied: "Well, the most significant source of happiness in life is having good relationships. Whether it is with people, animals, or the Earth. This is something I've learned over the years."

Roberto's simple but powerful statement reminded me that small acts of human connection can be acts of defiance. Civility, manners, and friendly public conversation are implicit ways of recognizing the interconnectedness of all human life. By taking the time to call elders on the phone or going out of our way to salute our neighbors, we help restore our society's tattered social fabric. The Black feminist bell hooks remarks how small interventions can aggregate into powerful forms of resistance. Reflecting on her upbringing in the Jim Crow South, hooks remarks that Southern etiquette and hospitality among Black communities exists as a way to combat dehumanization: "Simply by being civil, by greeting, by 'conversating,' we are doing the anti-racist work of nonviolent integration."[1]

Back in Tulsa, Oklahoma, Roberto helped found Cooperation Tulsa, an organization dedicated to healing relationships in a city torn apart by racist and settler violence. In 1921, white supremacists stormed Black neighborhoods, murdering over 300 people, injuring thousands, and burning entire districts in what is now known as the Tulsa Massacre. The founding of Cooperation Tulsa was preceded by another period of historic white-supremacist violence. In 2019, the police murder of George Floyd in Minneapolis led to major nationwide protests and unrest. Taking inspiration for its name from Cooperation Jackson in Mississippi, Cooperation Tulsa started a community organizing initiative to address this tumultuous period. At a local community center, the organization has provided free daily dinners and hosted community assemblies. With members from Cherokee, Muscovy, white, and Latino backgrounds, Cooperation Tulsa places multiracial alliance at the center of its work. Their first major undertaking was constructing a community garden at the Vernon African Methodist Episcopal Church, the only Black-owned structure to survive the massacre in 1921.[2]

Since then, Cooperation Tulsa has focused on developing community food sovereignty. On a 2.5 acre site called

Flat Rock on the outskirts of the city, activists have cleared industrial waste and transformed the land into a center for urban agriculture. The site, which is located on historically Cherokee territory, was contributed by a member of Cooperation Tulsa who inherited it from her settler family. Small, recurring financial donations from their community are used to purchase materials and supplies. In just a few years, Flat Rock has extensive raised garden beds as well as a drip irrigation system and storage facilities for other community garden initiatives in the area.

Emotional healing never figured into Bookchin's theory (indeed, he sharply criticized individualized models of self-help), but today it is common to many social ecology activists, figuring strongly in how they incorporate nonhierarchy into their day-to-day lives. One does not have to be fully emotionally healed to engage in this work (as if such a thing were possible). Indeed, embracing our flaws and committing to work alongside others and their flaws is inherent to the process.

REVOLUTIONARY EDUCATION

Education is a critical aspect of revolutionary groundwork. In today's anti-intellectual culture, intellectual development is often devalued and sometimes derided as "armchair activism." However, data show that group study is a critical form of collective action. For example, in a comprehensive study of grassroots Black economic power in the United States, political economist Jessica Gordon Nembhard examined hundreds of African American cooperatives from the nineteenth century until the present. On the surface, these projects were concerned with creating alternative economic relations. However, Gordon Nembhard found that nearly every one of these cooperatives originated in a study group or otherwise depended upon "the purposive training and orientation of members."[3]

Drawing on the revolutionary socialist and anarchist traditions, the affinity group (*grupo de afinidad*) is the baseline of revolutionary education in social ecology. Originating in the anarchist circles of nineteenth- and early twentieth-century Spain, affinity groups are small, highly personal collections of revolutionaries who convene regularly in a combination of study, leisure, and organizing. The affinity group is flexible, decentralized, and nonhierarchical. Together, the group organizes political activities, engages in collective study, discusses current events, critiques one another's writing and work, and more.

Participating in an affinity group is also a form of consciousness-raising and self-formation. Members must be dependable, consistent, self-disciplined, and accountable to the rest of the group. Regular group study habituates members to critical thinking, plain speech, and active listening. An atmosphere of openness and camaraderie allows participants to experiment with new ideas as peers. It is a critical way to form resilient and meaningful movement relationships.

Affinity groups shape participants into lifelong revolutionaries. As a young man, Bookchin dedicated over a decade to an affinity group led by Josef Weber, a German émigré who was formerly a leading member of the German Trotskyists. Weber's group, Contemporary Issues

(1947–64), consisted of approximately 20 members who met weekly at a member's home in the Bronx. There, they absorbed Weber's critical analysis of classical Marxism, which fundamentally helped shape Bookchin's own ideas about post-scarcity and the labor movement. The group began to discuss and write about new problems such as urbanization, environmental degradation, pesticides, and chemical food additives that other leftists at the time were scarcely aware of. Yet the group did more than political analysis. As the leading chapter of the Movement for a Democracy of Content, they sought to foment new forms of political organization anchored in the city or *polis*,[4] actively supporting the creation of town hall assemblies in South Africa and leading a global solidarity campaign for Hungary after the invasion of the USSR.

In 1951, Murray married fellow Contemporary Issues member Beatrice Appelstein, with whom he had two children. Although the two eventually divorced, they remained the closest of friends and political comrades, co-parenting their two children while co-leading study and affinity groups for the remainder of Murray's life. After Weber's death, Contemporary Issues disbanded, but soon Murray moved to Manhattan's Lower East Side, where he joined the New York Federation of Anarchists and the Congress on Racial Equality. Shortly thereafter, Bea moved downtown and together they formed a new group called Anarchos. Rubbing shoulders with the 1960s counterculture movement and New Left figures such as Herbert Marcuse, Sam Dolgoff, Abbie Hoffman, and the Yippies, Anarchos became a fixture of the Lower East Side's radical milieu. During this period, Anarchos started a journal and published Bookchin's influential pamphlet *Listen, Marxist!*, which sought to deter the subversion of Students for a Democratic Society, the flagship organization of the student-led anti-war movement, by authoritarian Maoists.

During this period, Bookchin reflected on affinity groups in his writing, describing them as a kind of extended family based on deep empathy.[5] As a decentralized and malleable form, affinity groups stimulate a shift in popular consciousness. In his view, this is essential to replacing the authoritarian aspects of the revolutionary party. Affinity groups provide "initiative and consciousness" in place of "general staff" and a source of "command."[6]

Bookchin continued holding affinity groups and mentoring promising young intellectuals well into his old age. Chaia Heller, who was one of Bookchin's closest students, moved to Burlington to study with Bookchin during the 1980s. In an interview, she reflects very fondly on her individual relationship with Bookchin, reflecting that although some experienced him as acerbic, he was incredibly attentive and caring to his friends and family. Toward his mentees, "Murray just was very generous of spirit. He was generous with his time. I was in my early 20s, writing terribly written papers. He would write over it line by line, editing for me. He just gave time and attention." With Murray's input, Heller would go on to develop a pedagogy of social ecology at the institute and write *The Ecology of Everyday Life*, which brings social ecology into conversation with feminist themes.

Over the years, Heller has maintained Bookchin's legacy as a mentor, hosting various iterations of a social ecology affinity group in Amherst, Massachusetts. On the heels of the Occupy Movement, I joined this group from 2010 to 2012. We would meet bi-weekly at Heller's home or at the shabby punk house where I lived with several of the group's other members. Chapter by chapter, we carefully read *The Ecology of Freedom*, preparing notes and reading key passages aloud. This particular group never evolved into an action group like some of us had hoped, but we developed a deep foundation in social ecology and formed lasting relationships. Notably, some 15 years later, nearly all of us remain engaged in radical politics.

Heller's individual mentorship fostered my intellectual and political development just as much as the group's dynamic. Like Bookchin, she spent long hours with me at her kitchen table, encouraging me to write down my personal observations and analyses and reviewing drafts of clumsy writing.

Heller taught me the importance of fostering a culture of gratitude and appreciation. She advised me, for example, to always thank participants for their time before a public talk or meeting. Ordinary people are busy and tired, she reminded me. To get to the meeting, they maybe have to take time off work or put off other engagements. "You've got to recognize that they're making a big effort to be there," she stressed, "because they have." Radical human connection is itself a form of praxis.

It is critical to have mentorship from people who share your experiences. The radical left can often be a minefield for young women. As I navigated this terrain, Heller, along with other women at the Institute for Social Ecology such as Ynestra King, supported my growth. They were generous with sharing stories from their youth and the practical lessons they learned from them. Mentorship from women who shared my experiences was critical to developing the skills to be an effective, patient facilitator or gracefully navigating challenging situations. Without this focused attention on my personal and intellectual development during these early years, I do not think I would have taken to social ecology as fully as I did.

Perxwede

Mentorship and group study are also critical to the spread of social-ecological ideas in Kurdistan, where it is called *perxwede*. During the 1990s, Turkish society reeled under high-paced, state-driven mega-development projects that devastated delicate coastal wetlands and traditional fishing communities. Public concern for ecology rose sharply, leading to several Turkish translations of Murray Bookchin's work. By the year 2000, there were at least two groups dedicated to social ecology, one in Istanbul and the other in Ankara, which joined to form a single group.

The group issued its own journal, each issue focused on a particular topic, such as the Anti-Globalization Movement, GMOs, or biotechnology. Their first issue, of course, dove into social ecology. Ömer, one of the group's organizers, remarks that the journal immediately sold better in Kurdish regions: "When we started publishing our journal, we noticed that it sold much better in Diyarbakir [the most populous Kurdish city in Turkey, often called the 'Kurdish capital'], so we doubled our print run in the second issue." The second issue's theme was nationalism, and the group translated a long article by Bookchin on the subject.

During this same period, the Kurdish Movement was concerned with the question of nationalism and the nation-state. Öcalan, recently captured and imprisoned on İmralı Island, was reading at a breakneck pace to identify viable pathways toward a democratic Kurdish sovereignty. When consulting with his lawyers, Öcalan always carried a book or journal in hand to signal to his followers to read that piece. *Toplumsal Ekoloji*'s second issue on nationalism was the first to make it into Öcalan's hands, who brought it to the next meeting with his legal team.

Before long, Turkish translations of Bookchin's work spread among Kurdish inmates in countless other prisons, including titles such as *The Ecology of Freedom*, *Towards an Ecological Society*, and *Philosophy of Social Ecology*. Bookchin's ideas were integrated among those of a suite of theorists, including feminist Maria Mies, Michel Foucault, and Immanuel Wallerstein, whose work was integral to *perxwede*.

In 2017, outside Hamburg, I had the opportunity to speak with one of these former political prisoners. He recalled that, although the guards beat and tortured Kurdish prisoners regularly, "they did us a favor!" by grouping all of the PKK fighters into a single, large cell where they were free to read and discuss revolutionary theory from morning until night. Eventually, the guards grew suspicious and separated these prisoners, but their studies and revolutionary fervor continued.

Tens of thousands of Kurdish political prisoners continue to fill Turkish prisons. The perseverance they show in continuing to learn and study while under immense psychological and physical violence speaks volumes about the strength and courage of the human spirit. It furthermore speaks to the power of consistent, face-to-face interaction. While bread-and-butter concerns are crucial, it is quite often the simple joy of existing in space together that keeps committed revolutionaries going. Visionary feminists emphasize that humans long for connection to one another and that this desire has disruptive power. By meeting regularly in affinity groups and committing to sustained face-to-face bonds, we fashion ourselves into people who are both ready for civic responsibilities and hungry for revolutionary change.

Hevaltî

Self-formation and relationship-building is far more important to the Rojava Revolution than many outsiders realize. Over the years, I have observed many presentations about the revolution by Kurdish liberation activists to an audience of Western supporters. I find these encounters fascinating because they often reveal widely divergent expectations about how revolutionary change comes about. Frequently, Western activists eager to understand Rojava's system ask presenters how democratic confederalism "functions." By "function" they mean how often various communes meet, how many people attend assemblies, how citizens calculate votes, how delegates communicate, how communes produce and compensate their workers, and so forth. They are looking for numbers, metrics, and structures that can be reproduced.

To the frustration of these audience members, Kurdish presenters often respond by diving into the revolutionary philosophy of Öcalan. They have little interest in – and little data about – the minutia of cooperatives, communes, or the militia units. Rather, they stress the attitudes, behaviors, expectations, and wisdom of the people within these projects. Although well meaning, many of these Western audience members have yet to grasp that what these revolutionaries are trying to convey is not a system that "functions" but a collective shift in consciousness. As the famous Italian anarchist Errico Malatesta once said, everything depends on what people are capable of wanting. The Kurdish Freedom Movement has achieved its gains by helping people think and act in revolutionary ways, a process they call cultivating a revolutionary personality.

Education, discussed in the previous section, is one key aspect of cultivating a revolutionary personality. Another is the practice of *hevaltî* or friendship. Rooted in the antique Persian word for togetherness, a *heval* (or *hevalno* in the plural) is a peer in the struggle, someone who has made a serious commitment to nonhierarchical relationships with others. In English, the closest approximation of *heval* is "comrade," which stems from the Latin "chamber" or camera, meaning a bunkmate. In other Romance languages, *heval* is similar to a *compañero* or *compagno*, someone with whom you share bread with ("com-" meaning with/togetherness and "pan" meaning bread).

As the chief form of address among guerillas of the PKK, *heval* conveys deep reverence and respect. *Hevaltî* is a life-and-death commitment for these highly disciplined fighters. In this context, a life of *hevaltî* calls for great personal sacrifice. Because of the Turkish state's ongoing war against Kurds, PKK party members must endure prolonged separation from their homes and loved ones, who are potential targets of government retaliation. Yet the life of a guerilla is also incredibly rich. Embedded in the pristine ecology of the Taurus-Zagros Mountains of northern Iraq, they teach one another Kurdish history, language, literature, folklore, dance, songs, and instruments. Members commit to months of intensive theoretical study, cultivating expertise on topics of special individual interest. It is a deeply communal, almost monastic, way of life.

Hevaltî means holding parity between men and women as an utmost priority. Since 1995, the PKK's women's units have had an independent command structure.[7] In their encampments, daily chores such as cooking and cleaning are split evenly between men and women, as teams rotate according to a carefully kept schedule. Sexual relationships between members are strictly forbidden. Many Westerners assume that this is a controlling practice. However, women fighters themselves regard the policy as liberating, noting that sexuality is one of the chief ways that patriarchal dynamics infiltrate women's lives.[8] The PKK's prohibition on sexual relationships is also an important gesture of respect for the villagers who make up their base of support. Today, a daughter who chooses to "go to the mountains" to fight for the PKK is an honor. Without the prohibition, the PKK would be seen as a corrupting influence on young women.

The spirit and practice of *hevaltî* extends far beyond the highly disciplined path of party members. Referring to someone as *heval* is a simple yet meaningful way to acknowledge their presence in a shared struggle. Civilians, activists, and supporters of Kurdish liberation everywhere invoke *hevaltî* as an ethos of mutual trust, openness, reciprocity, and nonhierarchy. Indeed, one of the most fascinating aspects of *hevaltî* is that it can be used in contexts outside of explicit political activity. Anyone can be a friend, regardless of one's personal history or ideological position. Kurdish feminist and sociologist Dilar Dirik explores this social-ethical world in her detailed ethnography of the Rojava women's revolution, *The Kurdish Women's Movement: History, Theory, Practice*. While *hevaltî* is embedded within political acquaintance, relations between people are multidimensional. Relations are "not mere[ly] political; many people are also relatives, partners, or fellow village or tribe members. Family-like bonds exist among people who lost relatives in the same incidents or visit relatives in the same prison cells or graveyards." In a society that normalizes individuals' alienation, people take joy in each other's presence. Dirik continues: "To many, the struggle is, above all, a sensuous, visceral space for collective healing and meaning-making."[9]

Personally, I have found the open and exuberant movement culture of *hevaltî* almost shocking in contrast to the austere and often insular atmosphere of Western activism. During my travels in Germany, Greece, the UK, and southeast Turkey, many Kurdish friends welcomed me as a *heval*, providing food, shelter, and practical help with unwavering respect, warmth, and regard. Several families extended open invitations to stay. Even though I was a young woman traveling alone, I was never sexually propositioned or objectified (an experience that any solo female traveler can tell you is all too common in other environments). In the presence of the friends, I have always felt safe.

Hevaltî exposes the limits of reciprocity as an ideal for liberated social relations. Reciprocity is premised on the idea is that we do things for one another's mutual benefit. We give knowing that we will eventually receive. But because reciprocity is based on the expectation of a return, it is still a form of exchange. In contrast, *hevaltî* extends even to people you may never meet again. In fact, it extends perhaps *especially* to people you may never meet again. *Hevaltî* invites a person into the stream of revolutionary life without conditions or expectations of return. It is a revolutionary generosity of spirit.

One small but meaningful moment is especially illustrative. I was attending a demonstration against the imprisonment of Öcalan in the city of Dortmund, while staying with a movement-affiliated family outside Bochum, Germany. The family had come from northern Syria only recently, having fled Islamic State with little more than the clothes on their backs and two small children. They had barely acquired furniture for their home, let alone the material accouterments most Westerners regard as "essential" to host, yet here I was. The day's demonstration was well attended but inundated with rain, and we arrived home in the evening soaking wet. As we walked through their front door, my host, Maha, a woman with beautiful brown eyes and short, dark hair, immediately disappeared to the bedroom and reappeared with a pink shirt and pair of socks. At first, I demurred, remarking that there's no way I could return them to her. But she insisted. Here I was, a stranger in Maha's home. And yet she was handing away her own clothing.

Tekmil

Self-criticism or *tekmil* is another technique for cultivating a revolutionary personality in the Kurdish Movement. Originating in the traditions of Marxist Leninism, *tekmil* brings members of a group together to address their individual strengths and weaknesses throughout a given period, usually over the course of several weeks. In the Marxist tradition, self-criticism is typically unidirectional. Party members are openly criticized by their superiors. *Tekmil*, however, enacts a more open and horizontal logic. The group is arranged in a circle and each participant is asked to assess their own work first. At this point, one can admit to mistakes, errors, or misjudgments and commit to improving next time. Participants are then given an opportunity to critique each other's work. When voicing criticism, *tekmil* participants are barred from critiquing an individual's character. Rather, they are expected to focus on the specific behaviors and concrete events that were troublesome.

Heval Tekoşin (a nom de guerre meaning "warrior-friend") is an internationalist organizer of Rojava's Diplomacy Center in the city of Qamishlo. In an interview, he revealed how *tekmil* and self-criticism helped him better understand his own domineering impulses. As a British national from a well-off family, Heval Tekoşin found himself frustrated when he first arrived in Rojava with what he saw as a lack of order and timeliness among his Syrian-Kurdish comrades. He hated how projects would not be completed according to schedule or how people would casually drop in and out of meetings and would often snap at his comrades. Eventually, Tekoşin's comrades shared criticism over his impatient behavior. Through the conversation, he realized that his strict expectations were largely a product of growing up in capitalism's production-driven mindset. Apparently, this realization is common among activists from the West who engage in solidarity organizing with the Kurdish Freedom Movement: "Our dominating spirit appears in unpredictable ways. We urge ourselves to be on time and to work hard. We hate it when things go wrong. We are hypersensitive to our own failures, and we often expect the worst from one another."

Over time, Tekoşin observed that even with missed deadlines or haphazard plans, people in Rojava come together when the task is important and that "somehow, everything gets done." Tekoşin's experience resonated with me and my own sometimes overbearing perfectionism. I found his last words on the subject particularly impactful: "The problem is not the problem. Our *attitude* to the problem is the problem."

REFRAMING CONFLICT

The human condition is defined by plurality. As each individual grows up, we formulate a unique set of experiences, preferences, opinions, and ways of interpreting the world. As political philosopher Hannah Arendt articulates this in *The Promise of Politics*: "God created man, but men are human, earthly products."[10] Radical friendship among those with whom we feel a natural affinity is an inherently meaningful form of praxis. However, the steeper challenge lies in cooperating with those with whom we are very *dissimilar*. Real democracy is a matter of figuring out how to live meaningfully beside people whose worldviews we do not always appreciate or understand. Differences in hierarchical society become axes of power and privilege. Innate human differences such as race, gender, sexuality, and cultural or religious background become terrains of struggle, from seemingly small indignities to systemic inequality.

The horizontal left has not been immune to social hierarchies. Even as activists try to eliminate hierarchy, old inequalities of class appear in how activists use terminology that folks cannot understand without secondary education. Inequalities of race appear in majority-white groups that select meeting locations that are difficult to reach from Black and brown neighborhoods, or by neglecting to consider parents or offer childcare – to name just a few examples. At a historical moment when systemic breakdown already creates serious obstacles to sustained movement, microaggressions, hidden biases, and less overt oppressive habits and attitudes inflame tensions and contribute to the collapse of countless promising projects and initiatives.

Struggles over interpersonal oppression and movement hierarchy have been painful yet generative sites of development in movement praxis. Joyful, an activist who has led several social ecology projects in the Pacific Northwest, now sees emotional wounds as front lines of struggle and transformation. Far from being a distraction from "the work," healthy conflict resolution *is* the work of constructing a society worth living in. During an interview, he passionately exclaimed that "*every single* activist project I have ever been a part of has fallen apart due to people's inability to handle their own trauma. Wounded people bring toxic behaviors into a space, which more wounded people react to. It is our single biggest issue." To help fellow activists heal from psychic damage, Joyful recently changed careers from emergency medicine to psychotherapy. He joins a growing wing of mental health professionals and practitioners concerned with the role of hierarchy and capitalism in mental health crisis. The internationally celebrated Dr. Gabor Maté links economic precarity and political instability to chronic stress. In family systems, chronic stress works in tandem with patriarchal attitudes and dynamics that normalize emotional abuse, neglect, and dissociation. Parents pass down unhealthy coping mechanisms to children. His work catalogs the now overwhelming research that undermines biological and genetic explanations for addiction, depression, and chronic anxiety, suggesting that these disorders are not inherited predispositions but rather maladaptive coping mechanisms.

New paradigms of transformative and restorative justice help people navigate out of the mire of internal conflict, teaching healthy conflict and conflict resolution as skills. Not long ago, "call-out culture" dominated the radical left. Born from a place of emotional reactivity, activists use shame and criticism to ostracize perpetrators of antisocial behavior, oppression, and interpersonal abuse within their own ranks. Although well intentioned, such reflexive use of punishment can be counterproductive. Transformative justice teaches us to work through the problems and controversies that spark conflict. Pioneering Black feminist scholar-activist Loretta Ross, for example, uses the term "calling in." When calling in, the purpose of confrontation is repair, not alienation.[11] Rather than disposing of offenders or denying/downplaying interpersonal conflict, they are given tools to better understand their own circumstances and how they themselves have been harmed by patriarchy and domination. As a leader of consciousness-raising circles among incarcerated white supremacists and perpetrators of sexual assault, Ross invites perpetrators into a deeper conversation about the systemic roots of their behavior. Although no rehabilitation process can guarantee that offenders will confront their behavior and change their ways, those who can change receive the appropriate support and rejoin the community as healthier individuals.

Transformative justice also prioritizes the needs of survivors. The current state-centered model of criminal justice does not meaningfully address the impacts of sexual violence and violent crime on their victims. Activists practicing transformative and restorative frameworks seek to reclaim justice from the hands of the state by foregrounding communities. Practitioners prioritize community ties and well-being, as well as early intervention, and ensure that harm is less likely to take place. Black and Indigenous women are often at the forefront of innovation in conflict resolution practices. Originating in efforts to end mass incarceration and abolish racist policing, restorative and transformative justice frameworks offer compassion and connection rather than ostracism and punishment.

In Detroit, Michigan, the Detroit Summer Programs led by Grace and James Lee-Boggs from 1992 until 1998 integrated transformative justice with an ecological perspective.[12] As the heart of the US auto industry, Detroit was devastated by the global outsourcing of the US auto industry. During the 1980s, over 100,000 auto workers were left abandoned and unemployed, the majority of whom were Black. Once thriving working-class communities were devastated. With the introduction of crack cocaine into struggling communities, poverty, addiction, and hunger went hand in hand, doubly so during this period characterized by the "War on Drugs." The Detroit Summer Programs responded to the crisis by organizing communities to grow food in abandoned lots and neglected urban spaces, reclaiming land, and creating welcoming green spaces. The Summer Programs especially mobilized Detroit's youth, who suffer multiple forms of violence under grossly under-resourced schools, failing social services, and racist police. Each year, Detroit Summer Youth Volunteers learned facilitation, active listening, and storytelling skills and how to address their issues without the intervention of police and jails. Building out through existing social networks and institutions such as churches, the Summer Programs prioritized the strength and quality of relationships over the number of people mobilized. This approach incubated a vibrant culture that blended public arts, community food production, and revolutionary activism.

People's Houses

In Rojava, principles of transformative and restorative justice can be found in Public Relations Committees or People's Houses. In these community-based judicial institutions, citizens can voice and resolve interpersonal disputes. Most of these disputes occur within or between families, friends, and neighbors, that is, people who have close and sustained ties. In addition to domestic conflicts, they can oversee economic issues such as petty fraud and failure to repay loans. Occasionally, they address serious antisocial behavior such as street violence and fights within the community. These entities lie outside the official state yet effectively serve as civil courts. According to activists at the Emergency Committee for Rojava, People's Houses have a 20- to 30-year history in many of the Kurdish-dominant regions of southeast Turkey, where local populations regard them as legal and political authorities.

Despite resembling conventional courts, People's Houses depart from conventional law and justice in several critical ways. In customary law, political authorities carefully codify societal rules that are universal and compulsory. Parliaments issue laws that police enforce, while courts and judges issue punishments for violating those rules, up to and including incarceration and, in many places, even death. This approach to social justice has little regard for context beyond what is codified in law. Judges may take pity on an individual in extenuating circumstances, but stealing bread, baby diapers, or insulin is just as illegal whether one needs these items to survive or not. The law is the law.

People's House committees approach each case as unique. Rather than treating everyone "equally," the committees consider the individuals involved and their particular circumstances. The Rojava Social Contract guides the committee in making its decisions. This living charter has been continually revised and updated through an ongoing popular constitutional process since 2014. In the Rojava Social Contract, principles of women's equality, environmental sustainability, economic justice, and respect for religious and cultural diversity are explicitly held in the highest regard. The committee's job is to apply these principles creatively toward a unique resolution for each case. Rather than establishing fault, the committee presumes a valid position on both sides and listens carefully to all of the individuals involved. The outcome is not so much a ruling but a mediation process that often requires action on the part of both parties. In an educational webinar about Rojava's community justice in 2022, Anya Brii, an organizer for the Emergency Committee for Rojava and an affiliate of the Kurdish Research Institute, remarks that the informality of the People's Houses may seem like a defect, but "if the purpose of conflict resolution is a harmonious society, then this is how we can achieve that goal. Their aim is to find an outcome that everyone can live with." In other words, the priority of the People's Houses lies in the satisfaction of people, not the satisfaction of law.

People's Houses operate through consensus rather than obedience. Before the dispute process begins, participants agree to honor the committee's decision, yet there is no means of coercing them and incarceration is not a possible outcome. If a ruling is disputed, participants can appeal to a central committee in the party office, which consists of two co-chairs, one a woman the other a man. While Rojava does have local police forces called *ayiasha*, they are largely tasked with handling external threats such as Islamic State sleeper cells.

Compared to conventional punitive justice, People's Houses have a relatively narrow range of sanctions available. However, social exclusion and ostracism are powerful tools. Echoing many traditions of Indigenous justice, the withdrawal of social approval creates pressure on an offender. Individuals banned from People's Houses are effectively excluded from normal community life. If a recalcitrant individual is a merchant, for example, their neighbors may no longer buy goods from them.

In Rojava and parts of Bakur, all-female People's Houses have special authority over domestic problems and other issues that disproportionately affect women, including issues of sexual violence, battery, harassment, character defamation, infidelity, and divorce. In the city of Diyarbakir, such committees have held men accountable for violence against their partners by seizing an abusive husband's job and transferring it to his wife, who would then receive his salary while learning valuable skills for employment. While her confidence grows outside the home, he is forced to understand what it means to stay and conduct housework. Interestingly, this communitarian approach echoes research by domestic abuse counselors suggesting that the single most important factor determining whether or not an abuser will change his behavior is his community's response.[13] The vast majority of domestic abusers never change because the surrounding culture makes excuses for their behavior or looks the other way. Patriarchal families and friends condone and justify the abuse by blaming the female victim, whom they blame for "provoking" or dismiss as crazy, dishonest, or blowing things out of proportion. The few abusers who *do* change are pressured continuously by their families and peers. By removing the tacit approval of abuse and openly shaming abusers, People's Houses erode the social conditions that lead to domestic abuse in the first place.

People's Houses are able to bring community justice through direct engagement and with individual committee members. To serve in this respected position, committee members must undergo extensive ideological training and study the Rojava Social Contract. Membership on committees is unpaid; however, it confers and reflects prestige. In this way, the People's Houses are reminiscent of the tribal justice prevalent before the intervention of nation-states in Rojava. In some areas, committees managed disputes well into the twentieth century. Elder male members of influential or high-status families would bring the families of aggrieved parties together to mediate disputes. Today, the People's Houses reject tribal honorifics or statuses and prioritize women as equal leaders. However, their justice ultimately rests on the wisdom of esteemed individuals within the community. People of the community recognize their rulings not out of fear but out of trust.

Community-based justice systems such as Rojava's People's Houses prove that we do not have to use the threat of punishment to coerce people into civil behavior. On the contrary, punishment only perpetuates intergenerational cycles of fear, shame, violence, and domination. Yet these systems are not effective in isolation. Community justice is impossible without trusting civic relationships such as *hevaltî*, self-improvement disciplines such as *tekmil*, or a pervasive culture of lifelong learning and study. Face-to-face participatory democracy requires a political culture that fortifies human relationships, trust, and forgiveness.

Revolutions are mental and emotional processes just as much as they are material or intellectual. On some level, every revolutionary is tasked with actively participating in a personal journey of healing and self-reconciliation. By getting in touch with our own grief, we can be truly compassionate toward the suffering of others. In this context, critique is not a distraction from the work, critique *is* the work.

CHAPTER FOUR

Creating Eco-communities

Every day, scientists make new discoveries about the creativity and consciousness of nature. In microbiology, we are learning about how forests communicate via microscopic networks of fungi called mycelia. These dense, intricate webs relay information throughout the topsoil in the form of chemical compounds. The roots of trees and plants then cluster around mycelia and use the information they convey to adjust metabolic processes and reallocate resources. In turn, these plants deliver food to the mycelium, forming a multispecies symbiotic network called the common mycelial network. Mycelial networks coordinate nutrients, carbon, and water cycles across vast areas. Remarkably similar to the neural network of a brain, they are crucial to the survival of entire forest ecosystems.

In ethology (the study of animal behavior), we are learning that many animals have a much wider range of perception, intelligence, and learned behaviors than previously imagined. Not long ago, it was believed that only advanced primates used tools. Now we know that birds, octopi, and other nonmammals use tools and very often pass those skills down to their young. Whales and porpoises similarly have distinctive habits that persist from generation to generation, including communication patterns, much like human language. Even among primates, the range of tool use is much wider than we previously thought. For example, scientists in Indonesia recently observed an orangutan applying a plant with pain-killing properties directly to a wound.[1] It seems that culture is not the exclusive purview of the human species.

This frontier of ecological science is more than just captivating; it is fundamentally reshaping how scientists understand what it means to be an organism. Paleobiologists now propose that the earliest multicellular animals emerged from cooperative clouds of bacteria. As evolution unfolded, these symbiotic relationships led to the complex organs and life systems we see in plants and animals today. Although we perceive life as individual entities, our bodies are, in reality, conglomerates of billions of microorganisms. Life itself is a testament to the power of mutual aid in action.

Insights into the depth of nonhuman agency are well known to the world's Indigenous peoples. In her study of the First Salmon Ceremony of the Pacific Northwest Coastal, Puget Sound, and Plateau Regions, Robin Wall Kimmerer documents how many Indigenous communities use seasonal ceremonies to collectively recognize plants and animals as participants in the creation of our world. During the First Salmon Ceremony, human communities gather around the swarming salmon as they travel upstream, only feasting upon the salmon once the ritual has been completed. In doing so, these human communities are physically replenished as well as spiritually galvanized. In turn, the salmon are actually shielded from other predators such as bears and eagles. Kimmerer regards seasonal ceremonies such as the First Salmon Ceremony as "reciprocal co-creations," where active recognition and engagement with nonhuman agencies are distinguished from abstract appreciation for nature promoted by the dominant model of Western environmentalism. Kimmerer writes that "[t]he feasts of love and gratitude were not just internal emotional expressions but actually aided the upstream passage of the fish by releasing them from predation for a critical time. Laying salmon bones back in the streams returned nutrients to the system. These are ceremonies of practical reverence."[2] First Salmon Ceremonies bring ecological processes and human cultures into a nexus of co-creation. They are just one of countless examples of such reciprocal relationships between Indigenous, peasant, and other land-based communities and their environment.

In this chapter, we focus on activist projects that work to restore these beneficial human–nature relationships where they have been broken. If all human societies prioritized the symbiotic relationship between humans and nature, critical philosophies such as social ecology would be unnecessary. Yet a just and sustainable resolution to the present crisis will require countless acts of ecological restoration from the heart of capitalism. In Chapter 3, we examined how social ecologists combat social and spiritual fragmentation through individual character development, radically democratic interpersonal relationships, and restorative justice. This chapter delves into how this same cooperative and nonhierarchical ethos applies to human communities and their relationships with nature. Often, these projects must emphasize the restoration of human–human relationships just as much as they emphasize the restoration of humans and nature.

PERMACULTURE

Enhancing the well-being of first nature is the central task of the permaculture movement. In this tradition of small-scale, decentralized, nature-mimicking, and holistic land care, farmers proactively compost and build soil, grow produce, regenerate forests, combat erosion, enhance water systems, attract wildlife, and enhance biodiversity. Practitioners Bill Mollison and David Holmgren coined the term "permaculture" in 1978 in Hobart, Australia, although over the years the movement has proliferated and diversified internationally. On March 29, 2023, I had the chance to sit down with Lisa Dipiano, a permaculture practitioner who helped found the Northeast Permaculture Network. Lisa got her start as an activist in the Global Justice Movement and is a former student of the Institute for Social Ecology. Now a professor in the School of Agriculture at the University of Massachusetts, Amherst, Lisa's journey helps us get a sense of how activists forge participatory and creative relationships with nature. Rather than tell Lisa's story for her, I reproduce sections of our discussion so she can tell you her story in her own words. I began by asking Lisa about the experiences that led her to become politicized:

I was very involved in protest while getting started in this work. My whole trajectory was through the Global Justice Movement and protest work. It started at West Virginia University, where I was going to school. I got involved in the Sierra Club and we went to parts of West

Virginia, where I saw mountaintop removal and talked to people who lived on the mountainside.

At that time, in West Virginia, you could count the number of environmentalists on your hand because the coal companies had such deep power, money, and resources. But we met folks like Larry Gibson. He would talk to anyone about mountaintop removal. He was not selling out to the coal companies. His family's homestead, he could trace his family lineage back through this cemetery. Larry was literally shot at and threatened for speaking out about mountaintop removal. He had bullet holes in his front door.

Thousands of acres around that site were once thriving forests. Whole ecosystems were gone. It shook me to my core. Once you see mountaintop removal, you can't unsee it. It made me realize the impacts of our fossil fuel-driven world that have been hidden from us. It also helped me put together how ecological and economic health are intertwined, and how poverty affects that. I talked to kids who had water pollution in their schools because of slurry ponds from the mining industry. I thought, "there has to be another way to meet our human needs without totally destroying the planet."

As a young political activist, Lisa joined the major international demonstrations of the Global Justice Movement (also called the Alter-Globalization Movement) against powerful transnational bodies such as the World Trade Organization (WTO), International Monetary Fund (IMF), and North American Free Trade Agreement during the 1990s and early 2000s. One critical area of focus for this activism was against ecological destruction or "ecocide" through biotechnologies and GMOs and the neo-colonization of the Global South. From 1999 to 2007, the Institute for Social Ecology supported the first Bio-Devastation Conference on genetic engineering organized in St. Louis, a series of counter-conferences and demonstrations around the annual biotech industry convention. Several students were also involved in the Direct Action Network, which laid the groundwork for a popular uprising in Seattle against the WTO's annual meeting in 1999, colloquially called "the Battle of Seattle." Lisa recalls the blending of reconstructive projects and nonviolent civil disobedience:

> This was in the late 1990s. The Battle of Seattle was happening, and people were getting involved in anarchist organizing, coops, and potlucks. I started connecting what was going on in West Virginia with what was happening in the world. The horizontal turn in social movements in the US. I got a taste of horizontal leadership in the assemblies linked to street action and decision-making, hand signals, learning all of that stuff.
>
> Social ecology was on my radar. Political street theater sprung up around 9-11 in response to the Iraq invasion and bombing. I was a part of a theater troupe that had formed at the ISE [Institute for Social Ecology] called the Liberty Cabbage Theater Revival. We arrived on a school bus that ran on grease. Murray Bookchin was there, Chaia Heller was there, and others. I took Earth Activist Training with [the renowned ecofeminist activist] Starhawk. We learned about direct action, and

Brooke [Lehman] trained people on affinity groups, spokes-councils, and assemblies. It very much connected these two facets: reconstruction and resistance in creating the world that we want to see.

I was part of protest hopping for a while. I went to Mexico [to the 2003 5th Ministerial of the WTO in Cancun], where we did a really fun action with [direct action trainers] Lisa Fithian and Starhawk. We used our privilege [and] disguised ourselves as Cancun tourists to get through the police line, and we had this code that everyone would gather and do this giant spiral dance right in front of where the meeting was taking place, disrupting the entrance to the meeting with the dance. At a counter-summit to a Free Trade conference in Miami, we also did a really, really free market at a public park to show what real free trade could look like. We were marching alongside farmers from South Korea and Guatemala. In disrupting meetings, we were building unity between union organizers and environmentalists, and we were building a global perspective.

As the Global Justice Movement gained ground against the IMF and the WTO, police repression intensified. Lisa found herself concerned about the limits of protest, which fed her curiosity about land-based approaches, such as permaculture, as a form of resistance:

When you really start to disrupt the power structure, you see that [here in the United States] we are dealing with the largest military in the world. The police in Miami were intensely militarized. They shot at us with rubber bullets, tanks rolled down the streets, and they gassed us with kinds of weird gas. We didn't even know what was in it. It became clear to me that protest alone wasn't going to get us to the transformation that we needed. Street tactics are not enough. That's how I got into permaculture and permaculture ethics – literally realizing the reality of what we are up against and the force behind it.

For me, entering permaculture was almost like a direct action, it was a way to literally start rebuilding a new world. In 2000, I went down to Guatemala, where I studied permaculture from practitioners. But I didn't realize it was a global movement until I came back to western Massachusetts and saw a flier in my graduate school for a training at an ecovillage in Shutesbury.

At that time, I was a renter. I had been learning about permaculture food forests. I took a PDC – a permaculture design certificate – the 72-hour course taught all over the world. It was a bit of a rite of passage, an intensive two-week immersive experience. We lived together, ate together, and went through the training together. For many, it was a profound experience.

In 2001, Lisa went to the Hampshire Anarchist Bookfair, where she met Institute for Social Ecology graduates Jonathan Bates and Eric Toensmeier, who would join her in creating the Northeast Permaculture Network. Together, they saw many overlaps between social ecology and permaculture, with both emphasizing interdependence, creativity, and mutuality. They started a web of demonstration sites, where ecological problems could be solved in participatory ways. They enacted principles such as the fair-share system, which distributes any surpluses beyond what one person or household is able to consume. Once one has achieved an abundance, you are compelled to give some of that abundance away. With these systems in place, they invited the public to see real-life evidence that countered the scarcity narrative. Lisa recalls:

> It started with a friend network going with a pickup truck and rounding up "waste" like leaves that people had raked and left on their driveways. We just connected informally. I guess today we would call it a mutual aid network. We would get excess woodchips from tree companies, using that to sheet mulch and build soil. We were also doing plant swaps and seed swaps. We reclaimed the tools that we had. We used cardboard, five gallon buckets and old pickle barrels – just whatever we had access to.
>
> We were really interested in building sites where people could experience these ethics and principles in action. People could come on and see, "Oh, humans are a part of nature! Or, oh, a problem is a solution." We started transforming yards and farms. Where once they saw a wet spot, they could see a rice paddy.

Lisa emphasized how permaculture principles connect to social ecology's principles of nonhierarchy, post-scarcity, and interdependence. These features attracted students and practitioners to the institute:

If you look at permaculture leaders in the northeast US, we were coming from the ISE. These were influential Global Justice Movement folks who valued non-hierarchy and saw that in nature. Symbiosis with plants, pest management by attracting pollinators – this ethos of what we're teaching that non-hierarchy is a part of that. Much like social ecology and the principles, the three ethics are (1) Earth care, (2) people care, and (3) share the surplus. With these principles, we try to integrate rather than segregate so that they meet each other's needs – for example, how we can integrate ducks with mushroom logs so they eat the slugs and produce eggs.

Crucially, Lisa notes that in building up ecosystems, they were simultaneously bringing together social networks and community:

When you look at the before pictures [of the demonstration site], you can see the land was barren, the house was burned down. Then you see later photos of ten people, gathering and talking. You are bringing people together; you are creating these really interesting ecosystems. You want to go outside and check on how it's doing, to see how it's changed in this season. You have a relationship and you are participating in it, also with other people. By building up these demonstration sites and making these really abundant places, by building up soil instead of depleting it, we were meeting people's needs and regenerating ecosystems.

Doing this work changes how you see on a visceral level. We used to joke about the red pill in *The Matrix*, saying it just changes how you see things. It's a new way of seeing people and ecology that gets carried over into other parts of life, into workplaces or politics. Or I joke that gardening is a gateway drug. You may learn about [this way of life] through gardening but then it becomes instilled on a deeper, ethical level where you realize, "Oh, land ownership and colonization! Gathering rights! I should be in conversation with the Indigenous people whose land I am occupying." Then you start thinking about reparations and how this new way of seeing and being is actually deeply rooted in Indigenous knowledge.

After building up the demonstration sites, the group's work became about teaching and creating the Permaculture Association of the Northeast. For years, they held a big summer convergence as well as regional convergences, working with students and practitioners from Montréal to New York City. Lisa remarks that there was a celebratory aspect as well. Throughout the day, workshops blended with socializing, food, and parties.

These days, Lisa finds herself reflecting on the mainstreaming of the permaculture movement. By building demonstration sites and sharing the surplus, Lisa and her companions invited others into a solidarity network and fostered a post-scarcity economy. But these actions alone could not address additional societal pressures such as making a living and securing healthcare. There was a paradoxical relationship where creating solutions led to popular interest, which major institutions such as universities have capitalized upon while leaving behind the movement's radical politics. She continues:

When you really start building these systems, it changes your life. You lower your cost of living and you can make a living from them. But it requires other people to live with you. You need people beyond the nuclear family. It's not a spectator sport! This way of life necessitates your participation, and it solves some of the problems we see with the nuclear family. The yard ended up letting Eric and Jonathan quit their day jobs. Jonathan eventually started a nursery because, as you know, perennials multiply! People wanted these plants and these seeds. Eventually, they sold their urban demonstration site to a land trust led by Black, Indigenous, and POC [People of Color] youth and mentored them on how to take care of it.

A lot of the activist folks, me included, ended up getting jobs as educators or authors. In doing so, we ended up getting absorbed into and brought into larger institutions. When you work 40 hours, you don't have time for it. I haven't been doing that here because I don't have anyone. It's funny, now that I have a kid, I have to tell her, "No, Esme, you can't just go into that yard and use that swing." It's bizarre to now have to teach and enforce that.

Today, the number of universities teaching this content is really high due to high student demand and interest. But how does it continue to be politicized? What really makes "permaculture" permaculture is that you can't just talk about Earth care without talking about people care. How do we keep it from being drowned out by the notion that this is just a cool farming technique?

The permaculture mindset that approaches problems as potential solutions supports this economy of abundance by teaching us to look for new tools. As our conversation wraps up, Lisa says she is optimistic about the possibilities of suburban renewal through permaculture, recommending David Holmgren's book *RetroSuburbia*.[3] The current model of suburban development is based on monoculture, embodied by the grass lawn. But, because of the relatively decentered allotment of land, and the presence of green space and waterways, many suburban neighborhoods are actually well equipped for small-scale food production, trade, handicrafts, and neighborhood production. If transformed into ecovillages, existing suburbia could be a cornerstone of sustainability and degrowth.[4]

COMMUNITY DEVELOPMENT

Lisa's experience of the permaculture movement shows how ecological restoration projects naturally engage groups of people. Community, in this sense, includes animals, plants, and all elements of the biosphere alongside humans. Dan Chodorkoff, who founded the Institute for Social Ecology with Murray Bookchin at Goddard College in Vermont in 1974, views social-ecological practice as centrally concerned with community development. His experiences during the 1970s as part of the Urban Homesteading and 11th Street Movements based in Manhattan's Lower East Side, nicknamed "Loisaida" by the neighborhood's Puerto Rican community, show how holistic community development can transform even highly urban places.

As a critical landing spot for immigrants to New York City, the Lower East Side has suffered from chronic racism, poverty, and unemployment. During the 1970s, entire blocks stood charred and empty as negligent land-lords found it more profitable to burn their buildings for insurance money than make them livable for residents. Local youth banded together to overhaul these neglected neighborhoods. Using green energy and sustainable tech-nology, they took over derelict buildings and transformed them into livable, communal housing. The movement cleared abandoned lots and turned them into community gardens, which became crucial habitats for insects, birds, and other city wildlife. Participants contributed to these projects via "sweat equity." In contributing one's labor, one gained rights and access to the spaces being created.

Urban gardens are common today, but back in the 1970s this work was revolutionary. In today's alienated urban landscape, we lack the social coherence neces-sary for meaningful democratic participation. The goal of the Urban Homesteading Movement is not simply to "regreen" the neighborhood but also to create the con-ditions for communal autonomy and self-governance. Neighbors who were initially attracted to the movement because they were interested in gardening or gaining new skills in carpentry or engineering grew more curious about communitarian ways of life as they became embedded in the movement. The gardens themselves invited new com-munity members into the process by providing a shaded, peaceful atmosphere where they could relax, chat, and get to know one another. "In creating physical environments,"

Chodorkoff emphasized to me during an interview, "we were also creating community."

In his essay collection *The Anthropology of Utopia*, Chodorkoff reflects on his experiences in community development. Chodorkoff is keen to point out how grass-roots community-building efforts dispute conventional understandings of urban development. Conventionally, development is understood as an economic process. Wealthy firms from outside the community are paid to bring in materials to construct new buildings and infrastructure such as shops and condominiums. But authentic community development is a holistic process. Social, political, economic, artistic, and ethical facets of the community integrate and strengthen the social-ecological fabric of a community. Even more progressive attempts at development can overstate the importance of the economy and finance. People need more than jobs or business opportunities; they need leisure time, access to land and public space, and a dignified way of life.

Alternatives that do not consciously and strategically oppose capitalism will eventually be absorbed by it. The modern metropolis, as an epicenter of commerce, is a site of primary concern for capitalism. As the Urban Homesteading Movement began to really transform the Lower East Side, absentee landowners reappeared and evicted activists in order to sell their properties. Without legal recourse, garden plots and housing cooperatives were eaten up by real estate investors and private capital. Rents and property taxes rose, displacing many of the working-class communities of color who led the Homesteading Movement. Paradoxically, by making the Lower East Side into a walkable, welcoming place to live – a rarity in New York City – urban homesteaders created the conditions for their own erasure. Today, the Lower East Side still has a handful of these community gardens, but little remains of their radical and galvanizing character during the movement's heyday.

Projects that showcase successful alternatives to capitalism eventually become targets of repression. Experiments in alternative ways of life must defend those alternatives physically, socially, and politically, as well as legally. Today, community gardens are a fixture of life in countless urban neighborhoods. However, for many low-income residents, they are now unwelcome signs of displacement and gentrification. I recall as an undergraduate university student in Richmond, Virginia, observing (primarily white) ecological activists struggle for a city permit for a community garden in the Churchill neighborhood, a historically Black community combating gentrification. Activists complained as Churchill's residents denounced their project at public hearings. In their view, residents didn't understand how the garden would improve their lives. From an outsider's perspective, it was obvious that it wasn't the garden per se that Churchill residents opposed. It was the gentrification and displacement that was sure to follow. Resistance, therefore, is just as critical to social ecology as reconstruction.

RESISTANCE IS LIFE

In the Kurdish Freedom Movement, there is an important slogan: "resistance is life." For the free women of Jinwar in northern Syria, creating eco-communities is itself a mode of communal defense. Embodying the ethos "resistance is life," Jinwar is an all-women ecological village and education center in the grassy plateau near the Turkish border. Formally established in 2015 on International Day for the Elimination of Violence Against Women (November 25), Jinwar ties together the themes of women's liberation, organic life, and self-defense. The village has built an ecological community centered upon women's experiences and political consciousness. It provides a place for women to collectively rediscover, re-establish, and reclaim their agency and identity without interference from men. It is the first experiment of its kind in Kurdistan.

On June 28, 2021, I joined a virtual conversation with the women of Jinwar hosted in collaboration with the Kurdistan Solidarity Network, a decentralized and nonhierarchical network based in the UK. Functioning without permanent leaders or offices, the Kurdistan Solidarity Network educates the English-speaking public about the Kurdish struggle while upholding the values of the Kurdish Movement in creative ways. During this conversation, activists from Jinwar stressed that an ethic of collectivity inflects everyday life. As one spokesperson puts it, "We do everything in a communal way, from the organization of the village, our lives and ourselves. This is a place of life, a place for creation and building up life."

At Jinwar, daily life revolves around organic agriculture and food production. The village is structured in a triangle shape, with a shared garden and common land in the center. Activists cultivate crops such as sunflowers, squash, tomatoes, radishes, okra, potatoes, and eggplant

in the garden. They promote and share skills in food preservation. Traditional grain varieties are harvested to make
bread, which is processed at Jinwar's own mill and bakery.
Jinwar additionally runs a public house, a general store
where local people can buy food and supplies, a children's
school, and a health clinic with its own ambulance.

Each of these projects is managed cooperatively,
without bosses or official leaders. Twice a month, Jinwar
holds an assembly of its adult inhabitants, consisting of
about 20–25 women. The women discuss their ongoing
projects and make plans for the future, implementing
an ethos of *hevaltî* and practicing self-criticism. Instead
of stressing the need for elaborate procedures, Jinwar
cultivates understanding and respect for each other's perspectives. One priority among the group has been hearing
everyone's stories, including traumatic histories of male
violence within families and marriages. Although most
of the women of Jinwar identify as Kurds, there is a great
deal of cultural and ethnic diversity among the women.
Their spokesperson explains this in terms reflecting social
ecology's principle of unity in diversity: "We have different
languages, different backgrounds, different cultures, but
we are building up a common life."

One key area of activity at Jinwar is preserving the traditions of the Kurdish village. For millennia, Mesopotamian
architecture has relied on mudbricks (*kerpiç*), even in the
creation of multistory buildings. At Jinwar, they revived
that mode of building, forgoing industrial tools to make
their own bricks by hand. They produce their own textiles,
such as wool, which is separated and spun in traditional

ways. These textiles are then used to weave traditional styles and patterns of dress, as well as create new ones.

Another one of Jinwar's main goals is to address the steep health impacts of oppression. The community clinic, Şifajin (women's healing) Health Center, combines natural, herbal, and modern medicine to revive women's knowledge and healing capacities, and to strengthen their knowledge about natural medicine and medicinal plants. In their worldview, health is relational. To be healthy "is to feel physically, mentally and emotionally well in relation to the society where you live." Health itself is a consequence of the way our society works. "The healthier the environment and the way of living and how the children grow up, the healthier society will be."

While most Western accounts of the Rojava Revolution view the Kurdish feminist militancy as new or unprecedented, the women of Jinwar see women's resistance as deeply tied to Mesopotamia's past. The region surrounding Jinwar has a remarkable cultural heritage, including archaeological artifacts with female and Earth-centered symbolism and iconography. Through traditional crafts, labor, storytelling, and cultural knowledge, the women of Jinwar defend Kurdish ways of life. The two most important symbols for Jinwar are the Mesopotamian goddess Ishtar (or Innana) as well as the thistle plant. Today Ishtar is referred to as a mere "fertility goddess," but ancient peoples in Mesopotamia believed her to control grain, rainfall, harvest, war, and protection. In the *Epic of Gilgamesh*, King Gilgamesh refuses Ishtar's sexual advances, wounding the goddess's pride. But in the Kurdish Movement's value system, the battle with Gilgamesh is motivated less by "pride" than by her desire to protect forests from patriarchal domination by the God Marduk. The thistle plant embodies a similar determination of spirit. A dry, thorny plant that thrives in poor soil, the thistle is symbolic of "pride" and self-protection while at the same time having a variety of important medicinal uses.

Jinwar's fiercely life-affirming and relationship-centered outlook is an expression of *jineologî*, the science or methodology of women. The primary goal of *jineologî* is to empower and revalorize women's knowledge, history, and epistemology, and it resonates with many forms of decolonial, intersectional, and transnational feminisms, striving to transcend the confines of traditional academic knowledge. Although the term *jineologî* was first proposed by a man, Abdullah Öcalan, Kurdish feminist and scholar Dilar Dirik insists that *jineologî* is collectively authored. It is a practicable body of knowledge derived from direct experience, storytelling, the interpretation of myth, and technical scientific understanding, "a form of knowledge production, and a set of methods for interpretation, a struggle for meaning giving, and an organizational effort."[5]

Advocates of *jineologî* see women as the original subject of colonization through marriage and housewifery. Therefore, the success of feminism entails not only the liberation of women but the liberation of society and life itself. In this way, *jineologî* is explicitly enmeshed in a broader program for popular democracy, cultural diversity, and ecological economics. Kurdish studies scholars Ahmet Akkaya and Joost Jongerden argue that *jineologî* is a form of identity politics that transcends the limits of liberal democratic theory.[6] By containing universal and particular claims simultaneously, Kurdish radical feminists maintain a dialectical "both–and" tension between the particular liberation of women and the general liberation of humanity as whole. For women at Jinwar, *jineologî* has as much to do with practices of reconstruction as it does with intellectual inquiry. In the words of one Jinwar inhabitant, *jineologî* is "the science of the living relations between living beings to each other. It is connected to our daily lives and the relations we are building up every day."

Jineologî provides a basis for women to deconstruct male dominance within the Kurdish Freedom Movement. This goal informs how Jinwar interacts with neighboring villages. Men are prohibited from living in the village, but they are not prohibited from visiting. "Actually, men like spending time at Jinwar!" a representative exclaims during our discussion. All kinds of people from the surrounding villages regularly come to visit Jinwar to help with construction and other projects or to chat, walk among the gardens, and be present. She assures me that "it is a village but it is not isolated."

Such informal, unannounced visits are a mainstay of Kurdish village life. During the winter, neighboring villagers regularly gather in Jinwar's common house to tell stories and watch movies. Borrowing language from Bookchin, the Kurdish Movement calls this village way of life "organic society." Life in organic society is lived on a human scale; one can easily walk from one's house to your friends' door, or a neighboring village is just a half-day's walk away.

By consistently interacting with the women from Jinwar, men from neighboring villages are changing their attitudes about women in general. In witnessing that the women of Jinwar meet their needs independently, such as by building their own houses and growing their own food, as well as by receiving medical attention from their healers, men's respect and regard for women has grown stronger. This slow, almost subconscious education process echoes other such experiences of male fighters of the YPG, who have served under female commanders. At first, these men resented being placed under a woman's command. But slowly, in witnessing their commander's strategic prowess – indeed having to trust their lives to it – the men learned to recognize women not only as "equals" but as potential authority figures deserving of respect.

Due to global climate change, such organic agriculture in northern Syria must overcome the serious issue of desertification. As rainwater grows scarce, underground aquifers are depleted and the water within them becomes more saline. In response, Jinwar has been improving its irrigation systems, planting trees in the surrounding hills to capture moisture in the soil. Similar regreening efforts are taking place all over Rojava. In the municipality of Derik (al-Malikiyia), the internationalist-led project Make Rojava Green Again convened local schools and teachers on International Women's Day in 2023 to plant hundreds of native, drought-resistant pine trees (*seru*).

Planting trees in Rojava is quite literally a way to defend life. Today, the land faces two twin threats: climate change and ecocide. In 2018, the Turkish military and its Islamist mercenary allies invaded Rojava's city of Afrin, cutting down and uprooting the city's olive groves. Hundreds of thousands of ancient and irreplaceable trees were killed.

This ecocide went hand in hand with ethnic cleansing. Before their invasion, the total population of Afrin was 85 percent Kurdish. By 2020, that number had dropped to less than 20 percent.[7]

The Rome Statute of the International Criminal Court regards ecocide as a war crime. Nonetheless, it remains a favorite tool of the Turkish military. In 2020, Turkey dammed the Tigris River to construct a major hydroelectric dam. In doing so, it drowned the 8,000-year-old city of Hasankeyf, along with over 1,200 towns and villages and an unknown number of precious Neolithic archaeological sites. This action was reminiscent of Turkey's war on the PKK in the 1990s, when the Turkish military burned thousands of acres of forests and agricultural fields to drive Kurdish villagers off their land.[8] By destroying the ecology on which Kurds depend, genocidal Turkish nationalists attempt to obliterate Kurdish cultural heritage.

Any day, the experiment of Jinwar could be annihilated by a Turkish ground invasion. If that happens, the YPG and YPJ will be there to fight and defend Jinwar and their neighbors until their last breath. Solidarity organizations such as the Kurdish Solidarity Network, Kurdish Red Crescent (Hevya Shor), and the Emergency Committee for Rojava will be there to raise hell with Western governments and campaign for policies such as a no-fly zone over Rojava. These organizations may not directly work with the land, but by providing moral support, sharing stories, and fiercely defending the right to self-determination and autonomy in Rojava and Bakur, they too take part of life-affirming networks that protect life and land.

Can Masdeu

At the ecovillage and social center of Can Masdeu (House Masdeu) on the outskirts of Barcelona, activists have found ways to align community development with resistance and opposition. Can Masdeu's story shows that radical communities can actually build their defenses by welcoming outsiders. Can Masdeu is a formerly vacated convent on the city's northwestern outskirts, a massive structure with stone walls and terraced gardens perched on the edge of a wooded hillside. On a clear day, the ecovillage has an incredible view overlooking virtually the entire city and out to the turquoise waters of Mediterranean. To reach the ecovillage from the nearest metro station, one must walk along a wooded trail. Along this journey, a cramped urban landscape gives way to shrubland and forest. The cacophony of cars and motorbikes subsides and is replaced by the chattering of monk parakeets in the treetops. Once in the shade, the temperature drops and the air itself seems to feel clean.

Every Sunday, Can Masdeu opens this pleasant world to the public. If the weather is hospitable, the events can attract over a hundred visitors. Many of these are activists and radicals struggling for change in the city center. Others are just ordinary Catalan residents looking for a respite. One main attraction of the open house is a hearty, plant-based lunch. For just a few Euros, plates are piled high with wholesome foods such as grains, lentils, and vegetables from the gardens below. Long, many-seated tables are arranged on the lawn, while inside an adjacent community room a small cafe offers modestly priced coffee, wine, beer, and home-baked treats. When I visited, the coffee provided was traded directly with growers in the Zapatista autonomous regions. The beer is brewed from the community's hops and they bake bread using wheat from the fields. After lunch, each individual washes their own dish with water pumped from the community's rainwater capture and irrigation systems. Clean compost toilets are available, which generate fertilizer to return to the gardens.

After lunch, guest speakers from social movements give various presentations, round-table discussions, and skill-sharing workshops. Many come from far beyond Catalonia, over the Iberian Peninsula, Europe, Latin America, and beyond. During my visit to Can Masdeu during a Sunday open house years ago, I gave a presentation about the resistance movements to hydraulic fracturing and other so-called unconventional fossil fuels. By meeting fellow presenters that day, I connected with the emerging degrowth movement and learned about Indigenous-led protests in Bolivia against Evo Morales' plan to construct a freeway through the Amazon.

Residents of Can Masdeu and volunteers offer guided tours of the premises. They share the project's history and explain the intricacies of their community living and con-sensus-based decision-making. They share how they run the gardens, grow food, and manage the surrounding forests, giving demonstrations about rainwater capture and identifying wild plants. Over the years, Can Masdeu has helped educate thousands of activists, providing a crucial node in popular education and material support for radical alternatives worldwide.

Can Masdeu is a nexus of co-creation between the eco-village and their neighborhood of Canyelles. In addition to the open houses, Can Masdeu gives their immediate neighbors free garden allotments on their land, which they use to grow their own vegetables, herbs, and flowers. This community rallied around Can Masdeu when it mattered most.

Can Masdeu is just one node in Barcelona's rich tapestry of social centers. In the late 1990s and early 2000s, Barcelona was a major hub of the squatters' movements that swept across Europe, occupying abandoned properties and turning them into social centers. These projects faced violent repression, with police successfully raiding and evicting many squats and communities over the years. In Barcelona, Can Masdeu stands out as one of the oldest squats, having been originally claimed by activists in the early 2000s. In 2010, it faced police violence when the city sent a SWAT team to evict Can Masdeu's inhabitants. When a core group barricaded themselves in the center of the building, neighboring residents came to their aid. During the perilous hours of the first night, when other activists might not have been able to reach the community, these neighbors left their homes to block roadways from being used by police reinforcements. The public's outcry dragged the attempted eviction into a days-long standoff, with police deploying smoke grenades and other devices to little effect. The people of Canyelles did not want the squatters at Can Masdeu to leave. Eventually, the police abandoned the raid and have yet to return.

There are literally countless ways for human communities to enhance the creativity and consciousness of nature.

As permaculture practices attest, we can learn to meet our needs while working with the patterns of a given eco-system. By approaching problems as potential solutions – such as by turning a muddy lot into a rice paddy or by transforming suburbs into self-producing ecovillages – we show that human ingenuity can be used to enrich and enhance natural ecosystems.

One of the chief ways we can learn how to work with nature is protracted observation. It takes time to learn the patterns of a given area or ecosystem. Indigenous wisdom often invokes an ample perspective on time. Yet one of the most insidious and pervasive evils of capital-ism is that it robs us of the luxury of time. We grapple day after day with the capitalist imperative to "earn a living," cut off from the rhythms of organic life. Meanwhile, our biosphere is changing rapidly. Defending ecosystems and lifeways from destruction is critical if we want complex life on our planet to survive.

Occupied social centers such as Can Masdeu aid in community defense by creating and supporting mutual-istic ecosystems of social movements. Their survival, in turn, often depends upon the willingness of communi-ties to rally around them when the authorities arrive to execute an eviction. In the French town of Notre-Dame-des-Landes, Europe's largest ecovillage or Zone to Defend (*zone à défendre*) stands on the site of a proposed airport. Local farmers are key to popular resistance against police eviction that has repeatedly rescued the village for more than 40 years. By grounding networks of social move-ment, land-based projects hold space for future protest

mobilizations and expand our understanding of community defense.

Land-based projects that steward nature and enhance
ecosystems are also an expression of nature's resistance.
As the Climate Justice Movement exclaims, we are nature
defending itself. Activists at Jinwar who cultivate heritage
grains and preserve mud-brick architecture are holding
the door open for a future where nature and society are
once again in harmony. For them, and other activists
in the Global South, building eco-communities is not a
matter of creating experiments or displaying alternatives
but rather finding ways to survive. Like the First Salmon
Ceremony, they create a nexus of nature, human communities, and cultures of resistance.

CHAPTER FIVE

Leading Popular Assemblies

For most people in the middle-class American suburbs where I grew up, the word "assembly" brings to mind teachers wrangling students as they file into gymnasium bleachers to listen to school administrators as they make announcements. In most United States public schools, these assemblies tend to be tedious and controlled affairs. They begin with a mandatory loyalty oath called the "pledge of allegiance" recited in unison. Administrators and teachers discourage students from speaking out or misbehaving. Assemblies of this kind are little more than communication events between managers and subordinates.

The stifling atmosphere of school assemblies actually reveals quite a bit about capitalist society's attitudes toward popular rule in general. Any activist can tell you that local governments often hide and obscure consultation periods when citizens are entitled to share their views on a proposed project. Dismissing society as too complicated to govern face to face, city managers and neighborhood planning boards tightly control ostensibly democratic proceedings in the hopes of getting through their agendas quickly.

In a directly democratic society, school assemblies would look quite different. Students would be given active and meaningful roles in their school and their education.

Their input would be considered invaluable to the future of the school. Similarly, teachers and staff would have a say in school administration as the management of their own working conditions. Parents, families, and the community at large would also have creative roles to play as former students and citizens in the enculturation of young people to a thriving democratic culture.

Public schools have often served as sites of communal assemblies in social movements. School gymnasiums and auditoriums are designed to accommodate large numbers of people. In many towns and cities, public schools already serve to delineate voting districts and are used as voting sites. They make ideal places to hold neighborhood assemblies. For example, the Urban Homesteaders' Movement in the Lower East Side during the 1970s used a local public elementary to hold quarterly neighborhood assemblies. At their peak, these assemblies drew more than 500 participants from around the neighborhood.

The beauty of assemblies is that there is a virtually infinite variety of techniques for conducting them. Nonetheless, there is a general pattern within this great variety. Usually, the group has already agreed upon criteria for what counts as a successful proposal. Most smaller groups prefer consensus decision-making, meaning that the entire group must revise a proposal until everyone is satisfied. Larger groups often opt for majority rule or a two-thirds majority vote. Leaders sometimes called "facilitators" take responsibility for moving through the agenda, as well as often publicizing the time and location and circulating an agenda in advance. Often, their role is purely as advisor and they abstain from the rest of the discussion.

The handbook *Robert's Rules of Order* presents a straightforward sequence of parliamentary operations, from a call to order, reports, recording of minutes, and adjournment. It also details motions such as tabling, recess, and points of order. Originally published in 1876 by an army engineering officer, this influential document is often regarded as the standard-bearer of majority rule decision-making processes in the United States.[1] According to state law in Vermont, for example, Town Meetings must use its procedures.

But many activists are also critical of *Robert's Rules*, taking issue with its emphasis on majority rule and confrontational argument. In recent years, democratic social movements have produced their own practical guides for initiating popular civic processes, including:

- *How to Win Back the City*, a guide for integrating social movements into a coordinated municipalist movement in a major city. Written by the citizen's platform Barcelona en Comú.
- *Handbook* by the Southern People's Movement, associated with the Malcolm X Grassroots Movement, a community-based organization in the US South.
- *Network?* by the Seattle Solidarity Network. This guide is about how to organize a workers' and tenants' mutual support organization.
- *Council* by the Portland Assembly. This zine is intended as a brief introduction to the Portland Assembly.

More than just guides for decision-making, they advise users on how to cultivate a genuinely popular process, collaborate with neighbors, and develop plans of action for issues such as housing, public transportation, and urban space.

Popular assemblies lie at the heart of social ecology praxis, yet they remain elusive and unpredictable. Small, idealistic groups of people can organize a study circle or a permaculture network but they cannot bring masses of people into the streets by sheer force of will. Historically, popular assemblies have often erupted spontaneously. In the aftermath of Hurricane Katrina in New Orleans and in New York City's Rockaways neighborhood following Hurricane Sandy, improvised neighborhood assemblies organized relief networks and mutual aid. As protestors in the Black Lives Matter movement have repeatedly confronted police and repression (Ferguson, Missouri, Baltimore, Maryland, and in many other cities across the US during the George Floyd Uprising), activists organized assemblies on the streets and in public squares. Impromptu street assemblies emerge during periods of crisis and upheaval.

Where committed revolutionaries have patiently organized underground, assemblies have helped usher in revolutions. During the late nineteenth century, thousands of members of the First International Workingmen's Association spent many months agitating and laying the groundwork for over 200 neighborhood assemblies in the working-class neighborhoods of Paris. In the spring of 1871, when the crisis of the Franco-Prussian War paralyzed the French government, they seized control and converted Paris, one of the largest cities on Earth, into an International Commune. Sixty years later, during the

Spanish Civil War (1936-9), anarchists in the city of Barcelona organized assemblies to govern and defend the city from Franco's encroaching fascist army. In the industrial neighborhood of Sants, worker cooperatives successfully fed over 100,000 people.

During the early 2010s, mass assemblies swept across the world, filling city squares, parks, and plazas with the demand for real democracy. Protests in Tahrir Square, Cairo (2011) led to the Egyptian Revolution and the fall of Hosni Mubarak after 30 years of one-party rule. In Istanbul (2013), protestors stood up to Recep Tayyip Erdoğan and his party's plans to demolish Gezi Park, one of the city's last green spaces. In Athens' Syntagma Square (2010) or Madrid's Plaza del Sol (2011), activists fought predatory banks and austerity policies that devastated working families after the 2008 financial crash. In Chile (2011), the Indignados Movement fought skyrocketing costs of university textbooks and untenable costs of living. Across the United States, the Occupy Wall Street Movement (2011) rebelled against bailouts for major banks while victims of predatory lending were evicted from their homes. The Movements of the Squares often flared up and dissipated quickly. Yet they fundamentally changed the political imaginations of millions of people around the world.

In this chapter, I examine how social ecologists have grappled with this powerful yet volatile political form. First, I discuss village assemblies as a means of stateless self-governance. In doing so, I try to decenter Western perspectives and demonstrate that direct democracy is far more than a middle-class conceit among youthful idealists. Second, I characterize social movement assemblies via my own experiences in the Occupy Wall Street Movement, where readers will gain a sense of how Western social movements have revived the assembly form. The remainder of this chapter looks at Bookchin's libertarian municipalism as an attempt to bridge these two worlds, fostering direct democracy as a means to build popular power at the heart of a capitalist empire. I focus on experiments in Barcelona, Spain, and Jackson, Mississippi, where the framework of municipalism has provided important lessons, insights, and interventions. Overall, I try to impress that while great strides have been made in the quest for real democracy, there is no single comprehensive blueprint or foolproof plan. The longer one finds oneself in the milieu of direct democracy movements, the more evident it becomes that nobody has all the answers and that direct democracy is always being reinvented anew.

A GLOBAL INHERITANCE

One of society's greatest conceits is that "democracy" was invented in the West. The prevailing narrative maintains that ancient Athens became the first true democracy when the aristocrat Cleisthenes established rule by the demos in 503 BC. However, archaeological evidence suggests that assemblies among the small, proto-Greek-speaking republics in the eastern Mediterranean had been commonplace for centuries.[2] In his ambitious investigation into the origins and evolution of democracy, *The Life and Death of Democracy*, historian John Keane suggests that the ideology and practice of democracy had likely spread West to the Mediterranean from Phoenician kingdoms, which in turn had adopted assembly-based democracy from Syria, Iraq, and Iran.[3] Direct archaeological records of assemblies date back as far as the first city-states of ancient Syria-Mesopotamia, where kings shared power with assemblies called *ukkin*.[4]

The legacies of assembly governance can be found in nearly every corner of the globe. In my own haphazard research, I have encountered accounts of directly democratic traditions in the Niger and Congo deltas of West Africa, the Sahara and the Arabian deserts, the Iberian Peninsula, the coastal regions of Colombia and Panama, the eastern Mediterranean and North Africa, in what is now the Pacific Northwest, the US southeast, Iceland, Lapland, Siberia, the Andean highlands, the jungles of Mexico and Guatemala, the highlands stretching from India to Southeast Asia, the German and Italian Alps, and the Tigris and Euphrates river basins, and of course the famous tradition of the Haudenosaunee in the North American Great Lakes. In a posthumous collection of her lectures at the Social Democratic Party School in Berlin, "The Dissolution of Primitive Communism," naturalized German revolutionary Rosa Luxemburg provides a global survey of relatively lesser-known decentralized societies based on assemblies (which she refers to with the German term *mark*), finding examples in Indian subcontinent, the Balkans, the steppes of Russia, and the Andean Mountains.[5] She finds assembly-style governance so commonplace, in fact, that she refers to it as a universal form of human society.

Assembly forms demonstrate a remarkable degree of similarity across vastly different cultural and historical contexts. In their history of libertarian politics in the

African continent, *African Anarchism*, Sam Mbah and I. E. Igariwey discuss village assemblies among the Igbo peoples of the Niger Delta. Their concise account provides a clear snapshot of how power moves from the bottom up in an assembly-based society:

It is the duty of the town crier, wielding his gong, to go around the village in the evening after villagers have returned from their farms to summon everyone to the village square at a specified time. The purpose of the assembly is often tersely stated. At the village square, elders outline an issue in detail and the people are expected to air their views as forthrightly as possible until a consensus is achieved. Neither the elders, the secret societies, nor the age grades [cohorts of boys and men charged with specific duties] could drag the village into a war or armed conflict without first consulting a general assembly for a decision.[6]

Mbah and Igariwey's account is remarkably similar to political scientist Guy Martin's account of assembly politics in Bantu-speaking societies in central and southern Africa in *African Political Thought*. Martin stresses that the role of leaders and chiefs is to facilitate the expression of popular will. When village elder councils could not achieve consensus, ordinary villagers "acted as the ultimate judge and final authority on contested issues."[7] Village leaders and elders are responsible for holding the assembly, but it is the group as a whole who ratifies all new laws.

Conventional political history disregards Indigenous traditions of communal assembly; however, they often lie at the foundation of resistance movements. Historians of the Haitian Revolution such as Laurent Dubois now argue that the fiercely independent political culture of West Africa was pivotal to the uprising. Rebel leaders orchestrated secret community meetings in the dead of night, speaking the Igbo language and practicing sacred religious ceremonies.[8] In *Intimate Direct Democracy*,[9] Black radical Modibo Kadalie looks at West African experiences with self-governance and how they factor into the establishment of maroon communities: independent Black and Indigenous settlements throughout the Caribbean and what is now the US southeast. For example, many captive Igbo and Ibo peoples were part of the Aro Confederacy, an economic powerhouse which controlled the entire Niger River Delta and was not fully subdued by the British until the early nineteenth century. Their liberatory political cultures feed into the directly democratic practices of Black-Indigenous alliances, maroon communities, Black-led economic cooperatives, and later of the Civil Rights Movement in the US South.

Bookchin looks to assemblies as the foundation of a future ecological society. In this, he is not alone. Influential socialist thinkers such as Cornelius Castoriadis, C. L. R. James, and Hannah Arendt have all helped clarify the role of direct democracy in revolutionary liberation. Tanzanian political theorist and politician Julius Nyerere saw village democracy as a cornerstone of African liberation from European colonization. Advocating for a systemic doctrine called *ujamaa* or "familyhood," Nyerere saw existing village assemblies as incubators of a uniquely African socialism.[10]

Despite the many virtues of popular assemblies, it is a mistake to think that their practice makes a society inherently democratic or liberatory. History shows repeatedly that the practice of assembly can be compatible with deep and persistent hierarchies of gender, age, and ethnicity. Countless assembly traditions exclude women, even ones tied to liberatory movements. For example, parts of northern Spain have managed communal lands, crops, and livestock herds since the Middle Ages in village assemblies called *consejos*. These assembly practices informed the radical sensibilities of Spanish anarchist and communist movements, yet since time immemorial, participation in *consejos* was a privilege denied to women. The Franco regime banned *consejos* in the 1930s as it stamped out political opposition. When I was in the region conducting fieldwork for my master's degree in 2015, I was pleased to discover that scattered villages in highly rural regions such as Burgos and Cantabria still practiced them. However, even today they are attended almost exclusively by men. Similarly, Switzerland is often looked to as a source of inspiration. The small country still drafts and ratifies legislation through a federation of highly organized, participatory cantons. Yet, incredibly, women did not possess the right to vote in that system universally until the year 1990.[11]

Patriarchal exclusion is not the exclusive purview of western Europeans. The militant Kurdish women of the YPJ and the PKK conceive their struggle as one waged on two fronts: first against the external violence of the Turkish state and second against the internal violence of male domination in politics as well as domestic exploitation and violence in the home. While it is perhaps impossible to parse what are the poisoning effects of European colonization and what is attributable to the local culture, there can be no doubt that women fight on the terrain of participatory politics just as much as their counterparts in representative systems.

The inability of direct democracy alone to secure social justice has been a source of criticism and skepticism about social ecology. Bookchin established his experiments in assembly democracy in New England, where assemblies called Town Meetings are still a part of local government. These Town Meetings often took inspiration from local Native communities who modeled direct democracy. Yet they were an inextricable part of European colonization and participated in military campaigns to drive Native communities from their lands. Understandably, today's activism calls for proponents of municipal democracy to grapple with ongoing legacies of colonization and dispossession.

THE COMMUNES OF ROJAVA

The quest to revive humanity's inheritance of assembly governance is not a call to relive a romantic past. Rather, it is a clear-eyed excavation of local democratic legacies that directly confronts their problematic histories. Today, in Rojava, local assemblies called communes provide a remarkable example of this. As the smallest unit in the Democratic Autonomous Administration of North and East Syria, Communes are intended to form the core of the political system and a key check against the centralization of power.[12] Each commune has several committees, dedicated to topics such as education, health, women, and economic development.

During my research from 2016 to 2017, I had the opportunity to learn about the communes from families who had recently made the journey to Germany from Kobanî, the city that famously defended itself from the Islamic State invasion in 2014. I learned that revolutionary ideology and communal practice around Kobanî are especially robust because of regional traditions of tribal governance, which some scholars argue are among the strongest in the world.[13] In this region, many villages are small, sometimes with no more than about 10–15 families. Even among these members, people often go to the cities to look for work. It is normal for these neighbors to meet in one house to chat and drink tea, especially during the summer. As one of my interlocuters, Azad, puts it, "In my village, people meet every day because they cultivate the land together and help each other. But, if there is a problem, then they say, let's meet officially."

In generations past, councils of male elders called "white beards" would resolve issues by bringing together adult male members of each household. Yet, women were prevented from participating in these forms for arbitration. Today, communes welcome all members of the community. Under the theory of democratic confederalism, each of these villages should have its own commune and its own delegates. These delegates report regularly to local districts and municipal councils, where they sit alongside delegates from dozens of other communes. Azad continues, "[Delegates from] my village do not go straight to Kobanî – we go to another town, which is the center of about 20 villages. Those 20 villages meet every month." On the council, members discuss, coordinate, share goods, and report on the outcome of discussions back at the commune.

One of chief means of ensuring women's meaningful participation in Rojava's politics is the *co-chair system.* According to this system, one man and one woman jointly hold every elected office, including delegate roles. Rojava also has a firmly established quorum for women's participation, meaning an assembly, council meeting, or voting procedure cannot proceed without a certain percentage of participants being women. The 2016 version of the Rojava Social Contract established a 40 percent quorum of women's participation at all levels of the elected government, while the 2023 edition of the contract names 50 percent.[14]

With participation guaranteed, women can turn toward deeper barriers such as ingrained sexism. One young woman I spoke with, Newroz, became an official delegate in her local municipality. As a delegate and co-chair, her job was to oversee services to over 20 towns and villages. She reflected that her fellow co-chair was a man in his fifties and initially didn't respect her but changed his mind after working with her and seeing her competence and enthusiasm.

Despite these remarkable accomplishments, Rojava's system of municipal councils and communes remains a work in progress. In many areas, the instability of war has disrupted the development of communes. In early 2018, Turkey's military, backed by Islamist militant groups in Syria, forcibly displaced the entire Kurdish population of the Canton of Afrin and replaced it with Turkish and Arab occupiers. In other areas, such as the Arab-dominated city of Raqqa, residents hesitate to participate in a system led by Kurds or instead prefer old party or tribal allegiances.

One key area of debate has been how to compensate people who serve as municipal delegates. Poverty in Rojava is currently driven by a three-sided embargo: to the south by Syria and Islamist militants, to the north by hostile Turkish state, and to the west by the ambivalent Kurdish Regional Government in Iraq. Much of the population relies on the central administration TEV-DEM for work and social services. Cooperatives and social enterprises are operational, but they are primarily operated by TEV-DEM rather than directly by communes. Yet, to avoid corruption, the civic administration TEV-DEM initially designated the role of being a municipal delegate as an unpaid position. As a consequence, many citizens lack the free time to dedicate to being a delegate. More recently, these positions have become paid – yet this feeds into a dynamic where ordinary people petition delegates instead of taking issues into their own hands.

Mehmut worked in communications for the Kobanî administration during the critical years of the revolution and was part of a PYD team that set about organizing some of the early communes. The group traveled from village to village to educate people about democratic confederalism, staging assembly experiments, several of which were tragically later lost due to attacks by Islamic State. Mehmut argues that TEV-DEM should be helping to establish more assemblies by supporting committed revolutionaries to

launch similar projects. While he longs to see more progress toward the utopian dreams of the revolution's early
years, he remains optimistic:

> We are now living only in the beginning of what could
> be a transformation. We are in a transitional stage.
> Nothing is stable. The view is not clear. ... Some people
> say we should empower the cantons, or indirectly make
> a state. Others are saying we should establish commu-
> nities, still others say that we should get the United
> States to support our infrastructure and support our
> diplomatic recognition. Inside this chaotic situation, to
> establish something like communes, you need believers
> and hard workers – in every single place, not just elec-
> tricity and social services. The Mission of TEV-DEM
> should be to give people power and to organize them
> with a very clear view of the present and the future.

Legacies of self-governance can be found in every corner of
the globe, but efforts to revive them need external support
and international solidarity. The difficulties of maintaining popular assemblies in Rojava should inspire activists
in the West to advocate on behalf of the revolution to our
governments even more vigorously. The US-based solidarity organization the Emergency Committee for Rojava
presses Congress to institute a no-fly zone over Rojava
and demands the cessation of sales of F-16 fighter jets and
other weapons of war to Turkey. These two small changes
in international policy would open up major possibilities
for the reconstruction of Rojava.

THE GENERAL ASSEMBLY OF
OCCUPY WALL STREET

Vladimir Lenin once famously said there are decades where nothing happens and weeks where decades happen. This was certainly the case from 2010 to 2013, when the Movements of the Squares, such as Occupy Wall Street, the Indignados, and the Arab Spring, brought mass public assemblies to city parks and squares across the world. Millions raised their voices against wealth inequality, political corruption, austerity, and the privatization of public goods and services. Crucially, these citizens were no longer directing their words to the government but to each other. The character of these mass urban assemblies differs drastically from intimate community assemblies. Yet they are crucial to the history and dialog of social-ecological praxis.

In the fall and winter of 2011, the Occupy Wall Street Movement and its encampment at Zuccotti Park/Liberty Plaza rocked the busy streets of Lower Manhattan. First established on September 17, 2011, the Occupy encampment served as a home base for mass demonstrations against corporate greed and wealth inequality. Within weeks, hundreds of similar encampments had sprung up in city centers across the United States, Europe, and beyond, joining New Yorkers in declaring "We Are the 99 Percent." By late November, police had evicted the protestors at Liberty Plaza and the vast majority of the other encampments, but the movement's political impact reverberates today.

I had the privilege of participating in the Occupy Wall Street Movement, including the iconic General Assembly at Zuccotti Park/Liberty Plaza. At the time, I had already begun learning about social ecology and direct democracy at a weeklong seminar hosted by the Institute for Social Ecology earlier that summer. So, when Occupy Wall Street erupted, bringing mass general assemblies to the doorsteps of Wall Street, I was awestruck. Deciding that I would not forgive myself if I missed seeing this movement with my own eyes, I quit my waitressing job and caught the Chinatown bus to New York City with two like-minded friends.

I heard the din of Liberty Plaza before laying eyes on it. Drums, chanting, police whistles, and a thousand simultaneous conversations about the state of our world reverberated up the sides of the surrounding skyscrapers. Lower Manhattan is a busy, bustling place, but with its towering skyscrapers, guarded lobbies, and overpriced corporate coffee shops, it is also uninviting and sterile. The encampment shined through with a vibrant energy – as if the park itself were alive. Here was a place built by humans for humans.

On the surface, Zuccotti Park appeared as a haphazard jumble of tents. It was mixed in with spontaneous yoga classes and a notoriously noisy drum circle. But a surprising degree of order lay within that seeming chaos. Activists, or "Occupiers" as we came to be known, had built an extensive public library, a staging area for painting signs and other artistic works, a medical tent, and an information hub with desks, computers, and other tech and logistical resources. The presence of countless police officers, cars, vans, dogs, and other apparatuses only heightened the riveting emotional atmosphere. The encampment at Liberty Plaza seemed to split the fabric of mundane capitalist reality. It was a true festival of the oppressed.

Each day, a General Assembly of the encampment was held at Liberty Plaza. This assembly was led by two facilitators, whose role was to guide everyone through the agenda. Each agenda item was announced, followed by a period of discussion, proposing amendments, and voting. General assemblies, spokes-councils, and working groups throughout the Occupy Movement practiced consensus decision-making. Through consensus, participants must collectively address all concerns and critiques via amendment rather than persuade a majority to support the proposal. In theory, this ensures that everyone's opinion matters equally and that nobody in the group is left unhappy with the decision at hand.

Facilitators relied on a support team of stack takers, time checkers, and "vibes watchers." Stack takers kept track of whose turn it was to speak next in assemblies. They would disperse throughout the crowd, noting raised hands to add to the list. Time checkers made sure the agenda was moving along, although this was often in vain. Vibes watchers observe the mood of participants and called attention to issues if people seemed frustrated or if things got a little heated.

Facilitator roles and techniques were complemented by a clever system of hand gestures, which allowed for rapid, direct communication among the whole group without verbal interruption. Wiggling one's fingers in front of you, or "twinkling," signified one's enthusiastic agreement with whoever was speaking without interrupting them with

applause. The same twinkling gesture pointing down-
ward expressed its opposite, a not so silent disagreement.
One could ask for clarification by holding up one's hand
in the shape of a "C" or hurry someone along by vigorously rolling your arms. One could even block the motion
at hand by holding one's arms up in an "X." Although this
was only meant to be used in the case of strong moral
opposition, the "X" gesture could result in the termina-
tion of a proposal. Hand gestures conveyed the collective
mood and gave an overall sense of where the majority
opinion was headed.

Occupy assemblies famously employed a technique
called the "human microphone." A speaker's words would
be repeated simultaneously by all in the vicinity who could
hear them, which set up subsequent waves of listeners to
do the same, and so on, until the entire crowd received the
message. Although cumbersome, the human microphone
allows huge crowds to communicate when folks otherwise could not hear each other. These clever democratic
techniques were meant to serve the practical function of
keeping the assembly. But, on a deeper level, they were
much more impactful by helping form a strong sense of
collective identity. In order to become part of Occupy, all
one had to do was learn a simple set of hand gestures. Many
of these techniques were handed down by seasoned activists from the Alter-Globalization Movement. The typical
occupier was in their early or mid-twenties, while activists
of the Alter-Globalization Movement were by that point
in their mid-thirties and early forties. These more experienced folks showed newcomers how to conduct general

assemblies, working groups, affinity groups, breakouts, and spokes-councils.

The General Assembly was powerful because it addressed people's long-neglected need for political expression. People naturally want a meaningful say in their own lives, yet nation-state politics deprive us of this. At Liberty Plaza, along with hundreds of other Occupy encampments, activists opened an *agora*, a space for public listening and hearing, for appearing and being seen. It allowed free equals to come together in mutual reflection about the human condition and the state of the world. People spoke passionately at general assemblies and spokes-council meetings because they deeply wanted to be heard.

Consensus techniques are not designed to handle daily decision-making among hundreds of strangers in a massive metropolis. Getting ten people to consent to the exact wording of a resolution is a long and delicate process. Getting 100 to do the same is impossible and, often, not even democratic. Young and/or wealthy individuals with relatively few obligations for work, childcare, or family responsibilities could outlast their peers in long meetings and have their resolutions passed without opposition. As the Occupy Movement's popularity grew, meetings lasted for many hours, sometimes dragging on into the night. When decisions were made, they were not always recorded. And even if they were, it was not clear how decisions would be executed. Eventually, general assemblies became unwieldy for even the most skilled facilitators, let alone the typical Occupy newcomer.

Another major issue was the reproduction of class, race, and gender privileges. During assemblies, it quickly became clear that people with social and educational privileges are more accustomed to taking up space in conversation. Occupy tried to address this through the "progressive stack." In a progressive stack, stack takers asked individuals to carefully assess their privilege and reflect on whether their comment was necessary before speaking. A pamphlet circulated at Occupy, "Structuring a Democratic and Prefigurative Organization Cheat Sheet," provides the following instructions for this practice, called "step up-step back":

> Notice how much you raise your hand and speak. Be aware of others who have not spoken and the environment in which they would feel comfortable doing so. If you aren't speaking but have something to add, assert yourself with the understanding that your comment will be heard and respected. Don't simply wait for your turn to talk, LISTEN.

Still, participants of color in Occupy repeatedly expressed feeling shoehorned into leadership or spokesperson positions while simultaneously not having their opinions or concerns taken seriously.[15] Occupy participant Sonny Sing poignantly remarked in *The Nation* magazine that when he read the Declaration of the Occupation of New York City, which proclaims Occupy as an alliance "formerly divided" by race, his gut reaction was that "this could only have been written by a white man." Despite Occupiers' attempts to be prefigurative, the inequalities of the old world crept into the seed of the new.

Practices such as the progressive stack and step up-step back are effective tools among groups of activists who trust each other. But the sudden popularity of Occupy was simultaneously its greatest strength and its greatest weakness. Driven by new social media technologies such as Twitter and Facebook, the Occupy Movement attracted newcomers who had little experience with the challenges of democratic movements. Because it grew so rapidly, the movement lacked shared political analysis, programs, and practical goals. With no criteria for membership or organizational processes by which to kick someone out, it struggled to maintain consistency, transparency, and accountability. Many activists worked tirelessly, burning themselves out. Others resented those who emerged as leaders and prominent voices in the media. These dynamics are troublesome for any movement but they are especially destructive to mobilizations that grow too fast.

Mainstream media and commentators like to remark that although Occupy reintroduced wealth inequality into popular discourse, the movement itself accomplished very little. This is often attributed to the movement's lack of specific campaign demands or unwillingness to organize a political party. Conveniently, these explanations omit the fact that police violence, encampment raids, mass arrests, beatings, harassment, and surveillance were major factors in the movement's demise. More importantly, these explanations miss the point. For all its flaws and contradictions, the Occupy Movement's goal was to demonstrate irrevocably that another way of life is possible.

A fellow occupier and Institute for Social Ecology educator, Brooke Lehman, captured this in conversation several years after the Occupy Movement. At the time, I was working as an organizer with the Institute for Social Ecology for annual talks, education seminars, and gatherings. Many former Occupiers participated in these events as students, fellow organizers, and guest speakers. Most of us rejected the notion that Occupy had "failed," yet we struggled to pinpoint exactly how Occupy had succeeded.

During one casual conversation about Occupy, Brooke remarked that since Occupy something seemed to be missing. Although she had already been involved in horizontal movements for years, Occupy was like stepping through a door through which she could not return. In the square, "it's like I discovered a part of myself that I didn't even know was missing."

Chaia Heller might describe that sense of longing and absence as political desire. Political desire is "an attraction, a passion, and yearning of oneself and for other selves." That desire is clear in the rich political biography of the Occupiers themselves. Former Occupiers have helped lead major mobilizations such as Flood Wall Street and the 2014 Climate Strikes and been on the ground for rebellions such as Standing Rock and the Ferguson Uprising. The democratic sensibilities and inclinations of Occupiers now appear in organizations such as the Democratic Socialists of America, which has a resolute libertarian socialist caucus, and grassroots networks such as Symbiosis and Counter Power. Occupiers have gone on to organize international solidarity for Rojava, Palestine, and other international liberation movements. Occupy has done far more than reintroducing wealth inequality into the popular conversation; it awakened in countless people a permanent desire for a better world.

The lesson of Occupy is not that direct democracy is too impractical to work. On the contrary, the lesson is that subsequent movements have learned greatly from that experiment. If Occupy's one-size-fits-all approach to democracy reproduced racial, ethnic, and linguistic inequality, we see today's radical municipalist movements prioritize multiracial coalitions and the centrality of non-Western perspectives. Similarly, if Occupy lacked social cohesion and a grounding in real communities, municipalist movements have prioritized place-based struggles and identities. Radical municipalists and fellow travelers have not abandoned the ideal of direct democracy. Instead, they have lowered expectations and delivered a more nuanced understanding of what real democracy means and how it can be achieved.

LIBERTARIAN MUNICIPALISM

Libertarian municipalism is Bookchin's program for how to replace the state with direct democracy using institutions of municipal government. He was intrigued by how municipal governments, which he called "vestigial institutions," often absorb remnants or fragments of self-governance from earlier periods of history. In New England, Town Meetings were once genuinely self-governing and to this day operate in tension with the state. He posited that a sustained, self-conscious citizens' movement could liberate vestigial institutions such as town halls, constituent consultations, and neighborhood councils and reclaim them for liberation.*

In that process, municipalist movements would put forward candidates in elections as spokespeople for the assembly. These candidates would not fill that public office as it currently exists. Rather, they would symbolize a collective desire to dissolve the responsibilities of that office down into the popular assembly. Should such a candidate be elected, it would be within the context of a revolutionary movement to abolish the role of the executive. In this way, libertarian municipalists seek to transfer popular legitimacy from the state to the revolutionary grassroots and eliminate the statist elements of municipal governance.

This approach takes advantage of the fact that institutions of local governance already have a degree of popular legitimacy and institutional power. The informal or "extra-legal" assemblies of Occupy might issue proclamations about public policy but they lack the institutional authority to immediately realize those goals. In taking over municipalities, a revolutionary movement would preside over public institutions, goods, and services such as hospitals and clinics, schools and education, health, public infrastructure, and the economy. They would also have built-in access to resources and relationships with unions, community-based organizations, and cultural groups. Rather than building entirely new institutions, libertarian municipalism aims to unleash the promise within those that already exist.

---

* By "citizen," Bookchin means *anyone* who lives in a given municipality, not only those whom the state deems legitimate citizens today.

Libertarian municipalism is also intimately tied to Bookchin's views of the city. In *Urbanization against Cities*, Bookchin follows the historical evolution of cities and their relationship to citizenship and the participatory management of the *polis*. Cities draw inhabitants together across diverse ethnic, religious, cultural, and linguistic backgrounds, bringing an ecological logic of differentiation to the social world. They are social watersheds. Throughout history, cities have served as incubators for vibrant intellectual, cultural, and artistic movements such as jazz, Dada, hip-hop, and punk, to take just a few recent examples. Fusions, hybridizations, and experiments are crucial to each city's unique identity and footprint. By bringing strangers from different backgrounds together, cities encourage inhabitants to think not only as individuals, or even community members, but as citizens responsible for the collective city environment.

Bookchin valorized the city not as it is but as it *could be*. In his view, the so-called big cities such as New York City, Tokyo, and Mexico City are not authentically cities at all but rather conglomerates or "urban belts" that need to be broken up and decentralized. In such metropolises, ordinary people derive a sense of meaning and belonging from their neighborhoods, sections, and wards. For example, New York City might be considered not as one city but at least five if we start from the five boroughs of Brooklyn, Manhattan, Staten Island, Queens, and the Bronx.[16] Libertarian municipalism channels the inherent social diversity of cities into a humanistic and ecumenical politics.

In the city of Burlington, Vermont, Bookchin found a staging area for assessing that theory. After decades of living in the vast metropolis of New York City, Bookchin looked to the New England Town Meeting as a living tradition of direct democracy. During this period, Vermont was a hub in the growing radical ecology movement, attracting environmentalists and socialists, including anti-war activist and fellow New Yorker Bernie Sanders. Bookchin and his inner circle dove into Burlington's urban activism, while Dan Chodorkoff and other social ecologists ran the Institute for Social Ecology at Goddard College, just an hour away.

In Burlington, Bookchin and his milieu's major experiment was the Burlington Greens, the first chapter of the US Green Movement. While visiting Frankfurt in 1982, Murray's close collaborator and ex-wife, Bea Bookchin, observed street demonstrations by the German Greens (*die Grünen*). On her return to the US, she suggested forming a Green group in Burlington. The Burlington Greens strategized libertarian municipalist intervention into Burlington politics through Neighborhood Planning Assemblies and City Wards. Candidates, including Bea Bookchin herself, ran educational campaigns for the City Council on a platform of direct democracy, ecology, and a moral economy. They organized opposition campaigns on a wide variety of urban issues impacting the lives of residents, such as the private development of the Burlington Waterfront and the expansion of the University of Vermont into residential neighborhoods. The Burlington Greens also introduced the idea of monthly Neighborhood Planning Assemblies throughout the city. According to Bea and Murray's daughter, Debbie Bookchin, these assemblies had a transformative role in helping people think through the issues facing their neighborhood. By 1985, the Green Movement grew to about 150 chapters and 200 affiliated organizations nationwide. At their peak, the Burlington Greens had dozens of committed members and received approximately 18 percent of the popular vote in municipal elections.

BARCELONA EN COMÚ

In recent years, a new wave of radical civic organizing has sought to reinvigorate radical notions of citizenship and the city, rallying around a common language of municipalism or *municipalismo*. Originating in the Movements of the Squares in southern Europe, particularly the Indignados Movement, municipalist organizations or "confluences" focus on urban issues such as housing justice, fighting urban megaprojects and redevelopment, combating gentrification, and protecting urban green spaces and public parks. Municipalist activist-scholar Vicente Rubio-Pueyo remarks that although the municipalist movement regards Bookchin as an important reference, there is no is no ready-made formula: "On the contrary, it is precisely under a specific political situation that certain concepts, traditions, languages, and methods acquire a new and fruitful sense."[17] *Municipalismo* throughout Spain builds on many decades of neighborhood assembly politics, including movements against anti-Francoist mobilizations, the Green Movement, and struggles for Catalan independence. The Spanish and Catalan term *municipalismo* likely arose independently from Bookchin's use of the term.

Yet it is worth noting that Bookchin himself was a committed student of these radical experiences. Barcelona was famously self-governing during the Spanish Civil War (1936–9). During the 1970s, Bookchin wrote a definitive English-language history of this period called *The Spanish Anarchists: The Heroic Years, 1868–1936*. This careful case study follows the rise of popular self-governance throughout Spain and ends with the Civil War. Bookchin's thinking about libertarian municipalism was shaped by his critical view of what he saw as the failures of anarchist organizations in Spain during the war, namely the reluctance of many syndicalists to formalize and empower neighborhood assemblies. He addresses some of those questions in a small essay collection: *To Remember Spain: The Anarchist and Syndicalist Revolution of 1936*.

Today's municipalism arises from decidedly modern concerns. In 2010, the Indignados Movement brought popular resistance to the Great Recession and neoliberal austerity to cities and squares across Latin America. In the spring of 2011, that resistance spread to Spain, where it became Quince-M or 15-M, referring to uprisings at the Plaza del Sol in downtown Madrid on May 15, 2011. The 15-M movement organized massive general strikes against the Spanish government's austerity provisions. At the height of the movement, popular assemblies involving thousands of people took place in plazas and squares throughout the country, such as Madrid's Plaza del Sol and Barcelona's Plaça Catalunya. Following these initial popular outpourings of popular resistance, the movement organized itself into large working groups called *mareas* (waves). Each wave worked to resist neoliberal austerity in public sectors such as medicine (Marea Blanco or white wave) and education (Marea Verde or green wave).

In Barcelona, tenants in the working-class neighborhood of Sants threatened with eviction had banded together to form the Platform of Those Affected by Mortgage Debt (Plataforma de los Afectados por la Hipoteca), the PAH. As European banks teetered on the edge of collapse, they swiftly recalled their debts from working-class people, who had only their homes as financial collateral. This resulted in waves of evictions and countless families being thrown out of their homes and onto the street. The PAH uses assemblies to anchor a city-wide mutual aid network to stop evictions through direct action tactics such as blockades. At least twice a week, they held assemblies where struggling families could come, share their distress, and ask for help. Through the assembly, participants could see that they were powerless against the banks individually but that together they had real power.

Barcelona en Comú, the flagship organization of the municipalist movement, emerged among former PAH and Indignados activists to hybridize social movements and institutional politics.

While conducting research in Barcelona in 2018, I sat down for an interview with a coordinator between Barcelona en Comú's neighborhood chapters, at their headquarters in the Diagonal neighborhood. When I arrive, the coordinator is eager to tell me about the history of Barcelona's vibrant social movements. Since the 1970s, he asserts, neighborhood assemblies (*asambleas de barrios*) throughout the city have struggled to develop their "force" (*fuerza*). Tired of seeing their initiatives crushed by hostile politicians in city hall, these activists decided to probe the barrier between social movements and local government. The idea behind Barcelona en Comú was to enable neighborhood assemblies to finally execute some power and enact reforms to make the city more hospitable to radical organizing.

In some respects, confluences such as Barcelona en Comú operate like conventional political parties. They design platforms, run candidates, and implement policy once in office. In the summer of 2015, Barcelona en Comú and Ahora Madrid secured major election victories. In Barcelona, housing justice activist and former PAH spokesperson Ada Colau became the city's first woman mayor, while Barcelona en Comú took 11 of 41 city council seats. In Madrid, another activist, Ahora Madrid's candidate Manuela Carmena Castrillo, a labor lawyer, was elected to the mayor's office. For the first time in over 40 years, neither of Spain's two major parties, the Partido Popular or the centrist Partido Socialista Obrero Español, would govern the country's capital of Madrid or the economic powerhouse of Barcelona. In office, Barcelona en Comú achieved a 50 percent increase in social spending and the expansion of social housing. In 2017, Colau's administration issued a moratorium on constructing new hotels and restricted new Airbnb licenses.[18]

In other ways, municipalist confluences act like social movements. Barcelona en Comú is made up of independent groups organized into a multilevel structure across Barcelona's ten districts and around 70 different neighborhoods. These neighborhood chapters have local autonomy. For example, their chapter in the Gracia neighborhood is called Gracia en Comu. Participation in these local chapters fluctuates depending on the election cycle, with membership swelling during elections as new policies, platforms, and candidacies take shape. Each branch represents the diverse characteristics of its immediate neighborhood. They are attentive to the social and political environment and address local issues and circumstances. As one municipalist activist in Barcelona's Gracia neighborhood put it in an interview: "If you participate, you decide."

The municipalist projects draw on the "right to the city" framework developed by French sociologist Henri Lefebvre and popularized recently by British-American economist David Harvey. Invoking this right to the city, municipalists assert citizens' rights to stay in their homes, access public space, and have their say in the planning process for their neighborhoods. They also disrupt major urban renewal programs that drive the displacement of poor and working-class residents.

One vital goal of the municipalist movement is to "feminize politics." Feminizing politics means realizing women's full participation and combating the marginalization and exclusion of women and gender-nonconforming people from public and civic life. Men's conversational styles tend to see the debate as a competition between ideas. One ostensibly wins an argument by persuading others to adopt your views by presenting a superior argument. Women's communication styles, by contrast, tend to be more conciliatory. Women look at others as peers and collaborators to be considered rather than as "opponents" to be defeated or corrected. In politics, a people-centered view of "winning" means producing a solution where everyone has their opinions acknowledged and their needs met.

Another key aspect of municipalist activism is the idea of "nonreformist reforms," which are provocative yet practical proposals aimed at opening literal and figurative space for even more radical transformations. One of the most well-known initiatives is the plan to create "superblocks" (*superillas*), which would close off small neighborhood streets to vehicular traffic and confine cars to main thoroughfares. Without cars, neighborhood children could play in the streets, residents could arrange plants before their doors, and people could bring out chairs into the street to chat. By reducing vehicular traffic, the city would be cleaner, safer, and simply more pleasant for residents. Not only has Barcelona en Comú succeeded in implementing superblocks in Barcelona but smaller towns in Spain have also implemented them, to overwhelming success. Residents report far less noise, less air pollution, a higher sense of social cohesion, and an overall improved sense of well-being.

Enric describes these efforts as the creation of a third realm. Invoking the metaphor of a beach, he says that social movements are like waves. "They rise with great force, then crash, and then rise and come again." Institutions, meanwhile, are the sand: constant and firm but malleable. Over time, waves can erode the sand, changing its shape and contours. "We are like those little birds you see," he says, leaning forward with a smile, mimicking the flight of sandpipers, "running back and forth between dunes and the waves."

Municipalism has spread internationally since its emergence in the Iberian Peninsula the mid-2010s. Confluences such as Barcelona en Comú have cropped up especially in eastern Europe and the Balkans, including projects such as the Initiative for Citywide Assembly (Iniciativa Mestni Zbor) in Maribor, Slovenia, The City Is Ours (Miasto Jest Nasze) in Warsaw, Poland, and Zagreb Is Ours (Zagreb Je Nas) in Zagreb, Croatia.[19] In 2017, Barcelona en Comú's international working group held an international convergence called Fearless Cities. From the meeting, a number of these organizations formed a Fearless Cities Network. In a plenary talk at the 2017 conference, Debbie Bookchin noted the power of assembly democracy to "transform, and be transformed by, an increasingly enlightened citizenry" who "by the very act of self-governing achieve ever-greater ethical character formation," which in turn guides the assembly "along the lines of 'rationality, community, creativity, free association, and freedom.'"[20] The following year, network members in at New York University and in Warsaw took the lead on follow-up convergences. Over 50 municipalist organizations are now united under the European Municipalist Network, an informal alliance dedicated to building resources, creating education materials, and strengthening this movement. From 2018 to 2020, municipalist activists kept a research observatory called Minim that has published hundreds of articles and reports about municipalist movements and aligned projects worldwide. Numerous other conferences, forums, and experiments in municipalism have been held in North and South America.

Not everyone aligned with radical urban movements or Bookchin's vision of direct democracy supports municipalist parties. In Barcelona, many activists, including squatters, anarchists, and libertarian municipalists, criticize Barcelona en Comú for putting energy into electoral politics at the expense of building neighborhood assemblies. Joan, a Barcelona-based libertarian municipalist who I met through our mutual involvement in Rojava solidarity activism, offered his perspective plainly: "Everybody in Barcelona thinks that they're radical, but really what they're living is social democracy."

Joan is a longtime resident in Barcelona's Raval neighborhood and an experienced squatter. Raval reveals a very different side of Barcelona than the relatively well-to-do neighborhoods of Gracia or Diagonal where Barcelona en Comú has a strong presence. As one of Barcelona's poorest areas, the streets of Raval are narrow; linens and laundry hang from lines cast between apartment blocks. Yet Raval has a rich and rebellious history. During the 1930s, it was home to trade unions of sex workers and career thieves. Nestled up against Las Ramblas, a major center of international tourism, this picturesque neighborhood has struggled against companies such as Airbnb, which absorb available housing, drive up rents, and displace struggling residents. In recent years, *manteros* – unlicensed street peddlers of trinkets, toys, and memorabilia directed at tourists – who are often undocumented migrants, formed their own union.

Joan invites me to a community lunch in an *okupa* in the Raval called El Huerto (the Orchard). The lunch is a fundraiser for Asamblea de Raval and their Committee du Defense de Barrio, autonomous organizations which protect against drug dealers, evictions, and encroachment of the tourism industry and Airbnb. The *okupa* is filled with raised garden beds and exquisite murals. For lunch, they pitch large tents and draw long tables into the square, where friends and neighbors mingle and chat. Here, Joan explains the reasoning behind his disillusionment. City police under the Colau administration had recently evicted another *okupa* in Raval inhabited by undocumented migrants. As the ruling party in the minority, Barcelona en Comú likely lacked the power and authority to prevent the eviction, but to Joan this was a sign that the movement had lost its priorities. Municipalists claimed to transform the state from the inside; however, in his view it is the municipalists who are changed as they accommodate the demands and rhythms of statecraft. Although he appreciates their motivations, "from what I've seen, every movement that turns to elections gets all their energy swallowed up by them, and they lose all their energy."

ECONOMIC DEMOCRACY

Material and economic equality pose one of the main obstacles to movements for direct democracy. Poverty prevents citizens from attending meetings and participating fully in their communities, while wealth affords a small minority of citizens' disproportionate political influence. Even the same municipality can see citizens living with vast discrepancies of wealth, making nominal equality and abstract rights virtually meaningless. This presents particular challenges to libertarian municipalists who seek to communalize the essential functions of the economy. What will a municipalist movement do with the neighborhoods full of mansions and the families who live there? What does it do with city centers constructed using the spoils of the colonial empire?

These questions become all the more urgent and complex in the face of social justice issues. Under modern capitalism, racism and material inequality cannot be disentangled. Should a social-ecological society seek economic reparations for the descendant communities of historical atrocities such as the transatlantic slave trade? And if so how?

The municipalist-aligned project Cooperation Jackson has sought to address the steep contradictions of our existing economy by building "economic democracy" or "solidarity economics." This project is based in Jackson, Mississippi, where the population is over 85 percent Black while whites hold 90 percent of the wealth.[21] To combat this staggering racialized wealth inequality, Cooperation Jackson has formed a federation of worker-owned cooperatives and other initiatives for democratic and ecological production. These cooperatives are integrated within a broader framework of communal production. Cooperation Jackson has built the Center for Community Production, a public community center specializing in 3D printing and digital production.

Cooperation Jackson has made its cooperative network accountable to the broader community by holding regular people's assemblies where their neighbors and supporters help determine and inform their priorities. At these consultations, Cooperation Jackson learns more about what kinds of activities will address people's needs. For example, with the outbreak of the COVID-19 pandemic in 2020, it became evident the city would do little to protect communities, and Cooperation Jackson scrambled to address the crisis. They were able to safely organize three people's assemblies, where citizens voiced their needs for personal protective equipment, which Cooperation Jackson then produced at their digital fabrication lab. Through this approach, worker assemblies or coops have control over their work conditions, while the community, organized as a municipality, has authority over major decisions such the quantity or quality of what is produced.

Economic democracy can take many forms. Cooperation Jackson is one member among hundreds of cooperatives in the US Solidarity Economy Network (USEN). USEN members experiment in community wealth-building and investment projects, participatory budgeting, cooperative development, and community-based production models. These groups are ideologically heterogeneous but their overall trajectory points to a growing desire for communities to control their local economies.

The labor movement has also moved toward a more holistic approach to questions about community and workplace democracy. The Labor Network of Sustainability has been pushing for a Green New Deal to combat the decline of labor unions, create sustainable jobs, and unify the climate justice and labor movements. Although historically labor-focused and community-focused organizing has been at odds, municipalism seeks to integrate worker empowerment within a broader framework of community assemblies.[22] By expanding their agendas, unions can operate as community organizations responsive to and protective of community well-being. We saw this during the late 2000s, when teachers' unions in the state of Wisconsin and beyond mobilized entire working-class communities, linking justice for teachers and school staff with justice for students, parents, and the community.

One of the chief arguments against direct democracy is its supposed inability to scale up. Much of this critique rests on the fact that today's globalized economy is highly complex. Infrastructures such as highways, national and regional power grids, global shipping, and supply chains rely on disciplined maintenance and oversight; discipline that direct democracy is unable to provide. Face-to-face assemblies may be effective tools for decision-making among small groups, critics concede, but some things just need to be centrally coordinated.

Practical concerns about coordination across large populations and complex systems are certainly valid. However, the vague notion of "centrality" conceals more than it reveals. State government, with its coercion and bureaucracy, is not the sole method of disciplined coordination over large territories. Confederations or federations (terms often used interchangeably) offer a decentralized model of social and political complexity. Under the right circumstances, they pose a practical and institutional alternative to the nation-state.

Federations reconfigure power so that it moves from the bottom up. Each participating assembly appoints one or more delegates, who are empowered to relay their collective decisions and voice their views. In Rojava, the co-chair system requires that two delegates be appointed at each level of government, with each commune appointing two delegates to the local municipality, and so forth, up to the highest regional level. In this way, federations are *rhizomatic*. Like a mass of roots, decentralized nodes form a larger, interdependent whole with multidirectional links.[1]

At their best, confederations are coordinative bodies rather than deliberative. A bottom-up and voluntaristic political culture encourages neighboring communities to directly communicate, share resources, and execute joint programs rather than appealing to a central political authority. Once a decision is reached, much is left to committees, working groups, task forces, and rotating sets of administrators, while teams of technicians, consultants, and specialists arrange practical details.

Delegates play a critical role in distinguishing federal politics from liberal representation. Rather than making unilateral decisions on behalf of the assembly, their role is to relay proposals, amendments, and decisions from the assembly to the confederal level. Among many federal societies, such as the Guna in Panama,[2] delegates are selected for their talents in rhetoric and argumentation. They are leaders not because they accumulate and wield individual authority but because they persuasively convey the will of the group. The communicative tasks of delegates are varied and complex – delegates present proposals, negotiate compromises, air grievances, share achievements, and call attention to potential problems. It is a highly respected and esteemed position, yet it can also be an arduous one that requires an inordinate amount of level-headedness, trustworthiness, and good judgment.

If a delegate is derelict in her duties, her mandate can be swiftly revoked.

Federations tie together all the many aspects of social-ecological praxis. Embodying the social-ecological principles of *unity in diversity* and interdependence, they foster nonhierarchical social relationships and provide a stage where sustainable practices and eco-technologies can be implemented on a wide scale. They provide an institutional container where individual eco-communities meaningfully associate in a broader network of shared humanity.

Because of that very ambitious nature, federalism remains one of social ecology's most challenging and unexplored areas. The Kurdish Freedom Movement is undoubtedly one of the most developed examples of confederalism in practice. In this chapter, we look at democratic confederalism in Rojava (or the Democratic Autonomous Administration of North and Eastern Syria) and in Bakur, North Kurdistan, exploring valuable lessons that Kurdish revolutionaries have put their lives on the line to produce. I consider these lessons in relation to historical problems of nationalism and identity that inspire the growing popularity of confederal politics. In doing so, I try to resist the temptation to romanticize federalism as a panacea to all the problems that liberation struggles face. Federalism is not a one-size-fits-all solution. Still, its growing international popularity speaks to a widespread desire to bypass dichotomies of centralization and localism, politicians and constituents, and insiders and foreigners through a logic of interdependence.

AN ALTERNATIVE TO NATIONALISM

To truly understand the twenty-first-century turn toward confederal democracy, it is important to look at earlier eras of global history and the international left. In the mid-twentieth century, as World War II led into the Cold War, European and US domination over colonial empires in the Global South partially disintegrated. Major socialist upheavals swept across countries as diverse as China, North Korea, Vietnam, Libya, Algeria, Ghana, Syria, Iraq, and Cuba, among others. Many of these national liberation movements were supported and resourced by the USSR and, later, China. Accordingly, they patterned themselves on Marxist Leninism and Maoist models, which relied on well-disciplined and often highly secretive vanguard parties. Intellectual movements such as Pan-Africanism and Pan-Arabism articulated promising notions of popular determination such as *ujamaa* and *ubuntu* but they were overshadowed by authoritarian parties. Thus, national liberation for the Global South became synonymous with state formation.

Many national liberation movements followed the path of single-party rule. New socialist regimes vigorously implemented domestic reform programs, nationalizing private industry, mechanizing production and agriculture, implementing land reform, and modernizing public services such as health and education. These programs no doubt generated positive material outcomes for millions of people. However, facing both external and internal threats, party leaders often tightly restricted civil society and stifled dissent. Fearing internal rebellion and foreign subversion, these leaders violently repressed their own citizens, especially cultural, ethnic, and religious minorities. Charismatic leaders and party chairpersons such as Muammar Gaddafi and Kwame Nkrumah became strongman leaders. Western governments secretly supported many of these figures to subvert and discredit the movements they symbolized. In Iraq, the US Central Intelligence Agency quietly supported Saddam Hussein for decades, contributing to the gradual collapse of Arab socialism. In the late 1980s, Hussein led a genocidal campaign against the country's Kurdish population, executing as many as 100,000 Kurds in the spring and summer of 1988 alone.[3]

Black revolutionary Modibo Kadalie lived this history through his experiences in the Black Power Movement. As a member of League of Revolutionary Black Workers in Detroit, Michigan, Kadalie was part of a coordinated effort to steer a groundswell of Black resistance against major automakers. Originating in wildcat strikes at the Dodge Main factory on International Worker's Day in 1968, the League seemed to signal imminent political upheaval for Black liberation. But by 1972, the organization had cracked and fragmented, as this intense period of mass action in Detroit as well as in many other parts the world ebbed away.

In a series of essay collections and interviews, *Pan-African Social Ecology*,[4] Kadalie reflects on the role of authoritarianism in the breakdown of the League. In his view, leadership became so invested in protecting its core vanguard that it ceased meaningful engagement with the broader populace. The League effectively cut off its own base of support. In a written interview following the book's publication, Kadalie explained to me how he arrived at these conclusions in more detail. He explained that the authoritarianism he takes issue with is not a matter of personality but a matter of ideology:

> In my own attempt to come to terms with what the mass upheaval in Detroit meant I realized that many of these elitist and hierarchal organizations were having the effect of impeding and literally corralling this vital living historical rebellion. Many saw this process as state co-optation. Of course, it was that. But contained within this co-optation was a serious ideological limitation. Almost all of the organizations that came out of this were offering solutions that would lead us right back into a reformed capitalist state in one way or another. Even those who saw the "capitalist state" as our enemy, saw the solution as some form of "socialism" within some form of the nation-state.

Grappling with these issues, Kadalie and a small circle of like-minded radicals who had been purged from the League started their own group. Meeting in Highland Park, Michigan, the group was composed of students from universities in the area who had advocated a democratic structure for the League's Peoples' Action Committee. The group was leaderless and made decisions by vote or consensus. He continues:

> We, essentially, became a study group of independent activists that were participating in most of the mass

actions in the area. The group did not require any allegiance to any prescribed "party line" but were free to
learn from their involvement in mass actions and
campaigns. There were no specific requirements for
attendance, although many people came and went. Even
so, attendance was very consistent among a stable core
of participants. The group met every Sunday morning
for four years and was a major part of the unrecorded
legacy of almost every aspect of the Detroit Mass struggle from 1970–3.

It was through this small group that self-directed
activists were placed in conversation with each other.
Because of the way we operated we had no independent
public profile. Consequently, we do not appear in the
record of that period as any Peoples' Action Committee. Many thought that we were "unorganized." But it
was fulfilling, and effective work.

The group at Highland Park worked in concert with fellow
Black radical figures such as Kimathi Mohammed,[5] who
circulated the historic study of Athenian direct democracy
"Every Cook Can Govern" by the visionary Caribbean
thinker C. L. R. James. In his own underappreciated pamphlet, "Organization and Spontaneity," Mohammed called
to reorient revolutionary Black leadership around the creativity and energy of everyday Black people. Arguing for a
"totally autonomous course of nationhood," Mohammed
insists that the role of leadership is to support the self-em-
powerment of ordinary people, not to direct them.

Today's stateless communities can look upon the
history of national liberation with the vantage of hind-

sight. Marxist Leninism's laser-like focus on central leadership and party discipline fostered a chauvinistic culture and attracted would-be dictators. Insistence on secrecy and obedience made vanguard movements prone to infiltration and collapse. Even when national liberation movements succeeded, authoritarian tendencies led to oppressive conditions that were scarcely better than preceding regimes. National liberation movements did not, as they hoped, transform the colonial state. Rather, it was the colonial state that transformed nationalist movements.

The failure of the nation-state paradigm presents stateless ethnic minorities with a new quandary. If state socialism and nationalism only reproduce inequality and oppression, what kind of movement can deliver real and lasting liberation? While we may never have a precise answer to this question, for Kadalie and many of his comrades, direct democracy is a good enough starting place. "Our first order of business," he insists, "is to wipe out professionalism ... Politics is not an activity to be undertaken solely by a small, privileged, and professional band of men and women. It must encompass the entire world body politic."[6]

DEMOCRATIC CONFEDERALISM

As one of the world's largest stateless ethnic groups, the Kurdish people stand face to face with questions of the state and national liberation. With the dissolution of the Ottoman Empire following World War I, the European powers divided Kurdish-majority regions into four parts: in southeast Turkey, along Syria's northern border with

Turkey, in northwest Iraq, and along the western border of Iran. For millennia, this rich and fertile land leading from the Taurus-Zagros Mountains down to the Tigris and Euphrates river basins has been known as Upper Meso-potamia, otherwise known as the Upper Fertile Crescent or the "cradle of civilization." This special region is home to countless ancient archaeological sites that shed light on humanity's Neolithic past, including the world's oldest temple and UNESCO heritage site, Göbekli Tepe. It is also home to a variety of cultural and ethnic groups beyond Kurds. Armenians, Azeris, Assyrians, Jews, Turkmen Syriacs, and Yezidis – not to mention Arabs, Persians, and Turks – all have deep roots in historic Mesopotamia.

Among these groups, Kurds have a distinctive culture. They are famous for their vibrant modes of dress, crafts and textiles, literature and fables, musical instruments, epic poems, dance, and multiple languages. Historically, many Kurdish tribes are herders who would migrate seasonally from the mountains to the plains during warmer months. The word "Kurd" first appears in a written form during the Middle Ages as the Persian word for "nomad." To this day, many Kurdish people living in rural areas distrust and avoid big cities and maintain close ties to village life. The Kurdish Research Center in Paris estimates that there are some 30 to 40 million Kurdish people worldwide. Approx-imately half of those individuals live in Turkey, while six to eight million live in Iraq, eight to twelve million in Iran, and two to four million in northern Syria. An additional estimated three to four million live in diasporas in Europe, North America, and Australia.[7] However, in the absence of official figures, it is difficult to verify this demographic information.

Because of their great numbers, strong cultural identity, and close relationship to the land, Kurdish people in the last century have been subjected to brutal exploitation and violence at the hands of surrounding states. The Turkish government has been at war with its Kurdish population on and off since the 1980s. During the mid-1990s, the military led a particularly vicious campaign to drive Kurds off their land, destroying thousands of villages and killing or displacing hundreds of thousands of people in massacres, razing, and aerial bombardments. In 1988, the devastating Anfal genocide saw Saddam Hussein use chemical weapons to massacre over 800,000 Iraqi Kurds within just a few months. The Baath regime in Syria and the Islamic Republic of Iran has likewise been harsh in their violence, exploiting Kurdish people as cheap labor, barring many Kurds from attending school, and repressing Kurdish cultural identity, economic power, and political autonomy.

Despite this overwhelming exploitation and erasure, the Kurdish Freedom Movement has posed fierce, multifaceted resistance. Originating in the PKK, founded in 1976, this movement seeks liberation for Kurdish people and their neighbors from the Turkish state as well as from global capitalism. For nearly two decades, the PKK upheld the principles of and methodologies of Marxist Leninism and Third World nationalism. While using guerilla tactics to stave off the Turkish state, they seeded revolutionary consciousness among Kurdish peasants and workers. As a typical national liberation struggle, their goal was to establish an independent Kurdish nation-state.

Gradually, the PKK's conception of Kurdish liberation changed. With the collapse of the Soviet Union in 1991, a world order in which Marxist Leninist groups such as the PKK could appeal for Soviet material assistance disappeared. By the mid-1990s, under Öcalan's leadership, the organization's views turned toward a more democratic and multicultural model. Moreover, it had become evident over the years that the standard socialist image of an industrialized worker's state made little sense among the decentralized rural villages of everyday Kurdish society. It was unclear how Kurdish nationalism could be squared with Mesopotamia's ethnic and cultural heterogeneity. A Kurdish nation-state would only substitute one oppressor for another, subjecting smaller minorities to the same kinds of persecution that Kurds have suffered at the hands of Arabs, Persians, and Turks.

Under the name democratic confederalism, Öcalan calls for a political system staked on popular assemblies and federations. Instead of struggling to create a fledgling state, Kurdish liberation activists cultivate de facto autonomy through municipal governments, participatory democratic institutions, and popular revolutionary consciousness. The goal is essentially to ensure Kurdish self-determination without reproducing the injustices and marginalization that Kurds have often been subjected to. At the same time, in the context of ongoing Turkish repression, Kurds can pursue a "third way" between an independent Kurdish nation-state and assimilation within Turkish society.

Democratic confederalism is an institutional container where a liberated society can flourish. Yet, like any container, it has little meaning without substance and content. Öcalan refers to that substance as "democratic modernity" or the "democratic nation."[8] Throughout this book, we have examined several examples of how revolutionary Kurdish activists foster democratic modernity. From eco-villages such as Jinwar to the everyday ethos of friendship, Kurdish activists foster egalitarian social relationships and embrace cosmopolitanism. A democratic nation, in other words, is a multiethnic and secular polity where all ethnicities and minority groups are equally respected and entitled to their own laws and customs. In Öcalan's view, the potential for a democratic nation in Upper Mesopotamia and the broader Middle East is far reaching. With its rich multiethnic heritage and legacies of assemblies dating back to the Neolithic, the region could be a flagship for federal politics in the twenty-first century. From the ashes of capitalist violence, a new era of human development could arise.

These utopian ambitions coexist alongside stark geopolitical realities. The state and statehood remain relevant for ethnic minorities because markers of statehood such as a passport and representation in international courts are the only immediate ways to secure human rights on the international stage. Sociologist Craig Calhoun calls this contradictory coexistence of state and nonstate aspirations *post-nationalism*.[9] Post-nationalism is a way of acknowledging that national identities are not natural or inevitable; they are created through systems of communication as well as through cultural processes, material systems such as roads, and education. Post-nationalism does not mean pretending that the nations aren't real or

pretending that state does not exist. Rather, it acknowl-
edges how stateless minorities are now looking beyond
the nation-state as a political solution.

Democratic confederalism has proven to be fertile
ground on which to cultivate a global post-nationalist
sphere. The Kurdish Movement and its supporters have
organized countless international conferences, academic
panels, webinars, solidarity campaigns, and delegations,
and visitations have been organized to explore greater
international collaboration and the sharing of ideas. There
is an ongoing collaboration and conversation between
Kurds and the Zapatistas as well as liberation movements
and radicalized stateless minorities in places such as the
Basque Country, Northern Ireland, and Palestine. Notably,
the only official political body to formally recognize the
Democratic Autonomous Administration of North and
Eastern Syria is the Catalan Parliament, which embodies aspirations for independence among Spain's Catalan
minority. The fact that these movements arise from very
different corners of the globe under very different circumstances attests to the fact that a change in thinking
is taking place. Centralized parties are receding as federations and alliances of popular civil society organizations
come to the foreground.

The neocolonial stereotypes of the Middle East see it as
anti-democratic and anti-modern. These stereotypes are
then used to justify Western domination, military inva-
sions, and seizure of the region's precious oil and natural
gas. The US invasion of Iraq was conducted under the
delusion that the Middle East needs to be provided with
democracy and its civilizing benefits. Democratic con-

federalism turns this assumption upside down. Invoking the directly democratic heritage of the region dating back to egalitarian societies in the Fertile Crescent, democratic confederalism reclaims democracy as native and authentic to the region. In the words of Pervin Yousef, a representative from Civil Diplomacy Center: "We want to see this multicultural system applied all across the Middle East. It is a revolution of the people, where all people can find their existence, together in a multicolor way." The people of the Middle East do not need to be "democratized" outsiders. Rather, they need to be unburdened from colonialism and the nation-state in order to express their own liberatory ways of life.

THE ROJAVA SOCIAL CONTRACT

In 2012, with the disintegration of the Syrian state in the Syrian Civil War, Kurdish-majority regions led by the PYD were able to shake off Baath Party control. Finally, after years of clandestine organizing, an opportunity arose to implement Öcalan's ideas of democratic confederalism. In the early period of the Rojava Revolution, the region was divided into three autonomous regions: Kobanî or the Euphrates Region, Afrin, and Jazira. Drawing from the language of the Swiss Confederation, these autonomous regions were called "cantons." From 2016 to 2024, the civilian arm of the TEV-DEM administration established several more cantons around the cities of Manbij, Raqqa, Deir ez-Zor, and Tabqa. In 2018, the canton of Afrin was lost to a Turkish invasion. Through an ongoing process of democratic deliberation and consultation with the region's many cultural and ethnic groups, the region was first named the "Democratic Federation of Northern Syria," then renamed the Autonomous Administration of North and East Syria. Each canton is governed through a combination of municipal and regional councils. District councils consist of 300 members as well as two elected co-presidents.

The civilian arm of TEV-DEM coordinates the various cantons at multiple levels and movement organizations, including cooperatives, academies, and communes. Launched in November 2013, TEV-DEM is an umbrella organization for democratic self-management and coordinates many core aspects of the Rojava Revolution, the People's Houses, Civil Diplomacy Centers, and the local communes. In some ways, TEV-DEM takes on the conventional competencies of a state, helping to coordinate and plan the economy and decide foreign policy. However, the institutions are meant to implement the people's decisions, not make those decisions for them, and what makes TEV-DEM different is the high degree of popular participation. In keeping with the principles of the revolution, it avoids the consolidation and solidification of political power.

A major task of TEV-DEM and the canton system has been to acclimatize ordinary people to a participatory way of life. This has been a long and ongoing process. For most people in Rojava, who had been subjugated by Baathist rule, the idea of self-management was utterly foreign. "This was completely new," asserts Pervin Yousef, a representative from Qamishlo to the PYD General Assembly at an online event hosted by Rojava's Civil Diplomacy Center in 2024, "We were always alienated from the power of our own decisions."

One of the major initiatives to introduce people to the democratic process is the Rojava Social Contract: a popular constitution that frames the people's revolution, its principles, and its procedures. The Rojava Social Contract is more than a set of laws. It is an aspirational document asserting radical democratic ideals and guiding principles for life in a post-capitalist, post-state society. The document declares Rojava as an integral part of Syria, guarantees political and cultural rights for all minorities, and honors the many thousands who have sacrificed their lives for democratic, ecological, and communal principles, as well as women's freedom. The preamble begins:

> We, the daughters and sons of North and East Syria – Kurds, Arabs, Syriac Assyrians, Turkmen, Armenians, Circassians, Chechens, Muslims, Christians and Yazidis – in our awareness and belief of the duty upon us from the martyrs, in response to the demands of our peoples to live in dignity, and in response to the great sacrifices made by the Syrians, came together to establish a democratic system in North and East Syria to form a basis for building a future Syria, without racist tendencies, discrimination, exclusion or the marginalization of any identity. Together, we resisted against tyranny, betrayal, and extremism, and we rejected all types of nationalist, religious, gender and secular fanaticism. Our adoption of the principle of the democratic nation strengthened our national unity, gave us strength in the face of our enemies and became hope for our friends.

The Social Contract of Rojava was designed using the very democratic means it codifies. As an initiative of TEV-DEM, a special committee authored the initial draft, which went through many rounds of changes and edits. In 2014, TEV-DEM shared an official draft of the contract among the different cantons, municipalities, and civil organizations.

Hundreds of face-to-face meetings took place as the document moved across the broader social infrastructure. The committee for the preparation of the social contract visited many places and aimed to see all of the different ethnic groups, even in remote regions. Special teams were set up to go house to house. At these consultations, care was taken to explain the technical aspects of the document and its principles. As the consultations brought together many opinions, debate swirled around key issues such as taxation, private property, and whether to remain part of Syria.

In 2016, after two years and hundreds of consultations, a revised draft of the social contract was ratified. This version emphasized cultural rights and the liberties for each group to practice their own culture, speak their own language, display their colors, and practice traditional arts. Cultural and ethnic minorities looked to empower themselves by organizing their own self-defense units. Pervin, from the Civil Diplomacy Center clarifies: "We have seen a lot of war and displacement, whatever ethnic group you were, you were suffering these things. Every group needed to build up their own organizations." In codifying cultural rights – rights which were extended to Syrians, Armenians, Arabs, and Yazidis – the Rojava

Social Contract shows that cosmopolitanism, internationalism, and multiculturalism are just as important to this vision of democracy as assembly decision-making.

In 2023 TEV-DEM released a new, updated social contract based on a decade of continuous consultations throughout the region. One of the major changes was to change the name Autonomous Administration of North and Eastern Syria to Democratic Autonomous Administration of North and Eastern Syria to emphasize cultural diversity and pluralism even more strongly.[10] This commitment to cultural pluralism has meant compromise in other areas. Women's liberation is a core value of the Rojava Revolution, with women's equality and liberation codified into the social contract, including laws relating to marriages and family. Early iterations explicitly banned domestic abuse, infidelity, and polygamous marriages. However, through the consultation process, Arabs concentrated in cities such as Raqqa and Deir ez-Zor have successfully petitioned to reinstate polygamous marriage as a protected cultural custom. Some might see this as the revolution failing women and girls; however, others see it as an acceptance of the imperfect, iterative, and contradictory nature of democracy.

In the early years of the revolution, Islamic State besieged Rojava, taking over large swathes of territory, starting at the Iraqi border. Where Kurdish, Yezidi, and other non-Sunni fundamentalist villages fell, Islamic State systematically slaughtered men of fighting age and took women and children as slaves. The people of Rojava thus organized the YPG and YPJ volunteer militias to lead their self-defense. From late 2014 through to 2018, the

YPG and YPJ led the successful effort to eliminate Islamic State from the region. According to credible sources such as the Rojava Information Center, 12,000–13,000 men and women fighters died in the process.[11] Despite this, the mainstream international community has resisted acknowledging the legitimacy and independence of the Democratic Autonomous Administration of North and Eastern Syria. The US military has offered limited aerial support, weapons, and other military provisions to the YPG and YPJ. However, no humanitarian or development aid has passed to TEV-DEM, the PYD, or any other civilian entity. Privately, Western leaders express sympathy for Rojava's plight, but publicly they fear raising Turkey's ire, a country with the second-largest military in NATO and the "gateway to Europe" for refugees from the Middle East and Africa.

AMED'S UNION OF VILLAGES

The Rojava Revolution in northern Syria has rightfully drawn international attention to democratic confederalism. The system there proves that a revolutionary praxis can thrive even under incredibly dire circumstances. However, Kurdish-led initiatives for democratic confederalism in North Kurdistan (Bakur) also have a great deal to teach us. In Bakur, the Kurdish Movement has created regional and national parties, such as the Peace and Democracy Party (BDP) and the People's Democratic Party (HDP). In 2015, the HDP secured enough seats to participate in the Turkish parliament, the first time ever for a Kurdish-led party. Yet these parties have aimed for much more than merely placing activists in office. From the early 2000s until the mid-2010s, these parties made significant strides by democratizing local municipal institutions. In the city of Amed, considered by many Kurds to be the de facto capital of North Kurdistan, the municipality helped to organize the Union of Villages, a confederation of delegates from neighborhoods across the city and dozens of surrounding villages.

Amed is one critical terrain of struggle. Amed is the city's name in the Kurmanji language. Officially the city is in the Turkish Diyarbakir. This remarkable city is known for its ancient ruins, including the Roman walls, historic mosques, and priceless religious and cultural heritage sites. In addition to historic architecture, the city is home to lively marketplaces and shopping districts, heritage food and bakeries, and lovely parks – locations that are brought alive by an active citizenry. Amed is one of the oldest cities in the world: its historic center, the district of Sur, is over 3,000 years old.

Amed is remarkable both for its ancient history and its present social movements. A deep love of social justice unites an integrated ecosystem of movements for grassroots democracy, ecology, women's rights and liberation, youth, and Kurdish arts and culture. The Kurdish Movement has worked extremely hard to connect these diverse grassroots projects, building a network of youth cooperatives and centers, urban farms, and women's cooperatives. They have created many programs to support and promote local arts, musicians, and performers. Organizations such as the Kurdish Women's Center help educate women on Kurdish history (Figure 3), and the municipality has employed people in urban gardening and baking. Community centers (*komala*) provide beautiful communal spaces, including much-needed green space and gardens. Women's centers employ women in economic cooperatives, where they are able to make their own money and become financially independent.

Figure 3   The Amed Women's Center, July 2015

From 2010 to 2013, the government of Amed instituted projects to weave the social fabric of a democratic nation at the city level. Embarking on a program of intensive historical preservation and architectural regeneration, the city government led projects to protect the city's ancient Zoroastrian symbols and statues, Jewish collective homes, and Armenian cultural sites. In 2010, a historic monument was erected in a local plaza to commemorate those killed in the Armenian Genocide (1915–16). As the first and only civil monument commemorating the Armenian

Genocide in Turkey, the project's symbolic importance cannot be overstated. Kurdish participation in the genocide generations ago is one of Öcalan's driving concerns in his conception of the democratic nation. The monument, therefore, represents a declaration of responsibility and genuine commitment to the multicultural principles that the movement espouses. Kurdish leaders expressed their deep remorse that Kurds took part in the killings and stated their uncompromising commitment to learning from these historical errors. Amed's then mayor, Abdullah Demirbaş, emphasized this point during our phone interview in 2015: "If we could face the past correctly together," he said, "we can face a true future together."[12] As mayor, Demirbaş also helped to convene a leadership council called the Council of Forty, bringing together religious leaders, including women, to foster interfaith dialog.

In the summer of 2015, I had the honor of staying in Amed and visiting its social movement initiatives. At the time the movement was focused on building up democratically organized villages and communes, via a convening body called the Regional Coordinating Council housed within the HDP-led municipal government. During my visit, a local activist group called the Mesopotamia Ecology Movement invited me to a special council meeting (Figure 4). Focused on advocacy for environmental justice in the bioregion between the Tigris and Euphrates rivers, the Mesopotamia Ecology Movement called for a meeting in Amed to address the significant ecological problems faced by the city and its surrounding areas, taking on issues such as the health of the rivers and the Ilısu Dam. Each neighborhood within the city and surrounding villages held an assembly in preparation for the confederal meeting and selected their delegates according to the co-chair system. Each delegation consisted of one woman and one man. The role of these delegates was to communicate the community's wishes and desires. Any major decisions would be brought back down to the local assembly.

Figure 4   Union of Municipalities meeting, Amed

At the council, some 50 to 60 delegates came together in a modern convention hall on the outskirts of city. Representatives from the Mesopotamia Ecology Movement, the council, and other social movement organizations attended and helped facilitate the discussion. The primary topic was water quality along the Tigris. Due to climate change, crop irrigation is becoming more difficult, and more precious water is being siphoned off by struggling farmers. The community discussed plans for reforesting the countryside, creating urban green spaces, planting orchards, and cultivating local food self-sufficiency.

One delegate sticks out in my memory as embodying the personal leadership qualities of eloquence, compassion, listening skills, and negotiation. Hailing from a small village outside Amed, he argued passionately about the need to bring the confederation from the city center to the countryside. While most speakers wore modern clothes or even suits, this gentleman, who appeared to be in his late sixties, was dressed in a simple cotton tunic. By voicing a critique and having that critique acknowledged, respected, and addressed, he showed the dialectic of democracy at work.

In 2016, President Erdoğan reignited the war against the Kurds, targeting Amed. HDP activists and politicians were imprisoned, community centers were raided and shut down, and the movement for local autonomy was driven underground. The Turkish police forcibly disbanded the Regional Coordinating Council, imprisoned the activists who hosted me at Amed's Women's Center and raided the Kurdish-majority HDP offices. Several of the comrades who hosted me eventually had to leave the country while entire sections of Amed were destroyed by bombardment, including the ancient district of Sur. The Union of Villages was also among the dozens of organizations disbanded.

Yet this war was just another link in a long chain of Turkish state violence. Turkey consistently ranks among the top human rights abusers according to human rights organizations such as the European Court of Human Rights.[13] Since the early 1990s, the Turkish government has killed well over 40,000 Kurdish civilians in Bakur. Even speaking Kurmanji, the Kurdish language, is forbidden in government buildings. In 2013, Abdullah Demirbaş, the mayor who oversaw Amed's Armenian Genocide Monument, was imprisoned in a sweep of the BDP leadership. The HDP was duly elected to the Turkish parliament in 2015. The following year, the party was abolished and its leadership was thrown into prison, including Selahattin Demirtaş, the HDP's 2014 presidential candidate, who has remained in prison ever since. Despite these years of violent repression, the Bakuri people have never given up their struggle.

Since the destruction of Amed, I have often wondered what happened to the man who represented his small village. Was he able to realize his goal of a confederal meeting based in the villages? The tragic and unjust destruction in Amed raises the question of what might be possible without such overwhelming violence and repression. In retrospect, it is clear to me why Erdoğan, a man desperate to project power, took such extreme measures. He did so because democratic confederalism was working.

THE ZAPATISTAS AND BEYOND

One of the critical features of the Rojava Revolution is creativity and invention as inherent features of its democratic process. Democratic confederalism cannot be reduced to any particular individual's vision, be it Öcalan's, Bookchin's, or anyone else's. Indeed, federal politics are already deeply woven into the political histories of many Indigenous peoples throughout the world. The Six Nations of the Haudenosaunee, an alliance of six independent tribal groups, oversaw centuries of peaceful coexistence in what is now the northeast and north-central United States (Turtle Island). In other parts of Turtle Island, similar tribal confederacies such as the Blackfoot Confederacy, the Pontiac Confederacy, the Powhatan Confederacy, the Muscogee-Creek Confederacy, and the Illinois Confederacy were just as prominent before, during, and after European colonization.

Indigenous horizontal practices forms are not reducible to Western conceptions of direct democracy. In her ethnographic work in Peru, Ecuador, and Bolivia, anthropologist Marisol de la Cadena analyzes how Andean Quechua speakers invoke ecosystems such as mountains and rivers as willful agents and authentic participants – "Earth Beings" – within community deliberations.[14] De la Cadena argues that, by conjuring nonhumans as actors in the political arena, Indigenous "cosmopolitics" exceeds the conceptual boundaries of Western politics. Many Indigenous political traditions draw themes of nature and the nonhuman into community deliberation. Western rationalism regards these "spiritual" or "religious" rituals as transgressions of secular deliberation. That is, they introduce the personal or the subjective into what should be an objective process. But Latin American and Indigenous scholars show us that another way to view the close integration of community deliberation and spiritual ritual and symbolism is regarding humanity's position as a nature-made consciousness.

The Zapatista Army of National Liberation (EZLN) in Chiapas, Mexico, articulates this message of incommensurability in their communications with the outside world. Based in Mexico's southernmost region, the Zapatista Movement is a historic synthesis of Indigenous autonomy and global left politics. The EZLN was formed from a decades-long process of dialog between the predominantly mestizo membership of the Marxist Leninist guerrilla party Forces of National Liberation (FLN) and the Indigenous Mayan peoples of the Lacandon jungle. In a story reminiscent of the PKK, in 1983 members of the FLN took to the mountains to prepare for an armed struggle with the Mexican state. Although their intention was to radicalize the local population, instead they discovered that the local Mayan people were already practicing community assemblies formed through an influential regional history of liberation theology, revolutionary Maoism, and pre-Columbian Mayan self-management. Over the next decade, these members of the FLN became the EZLN and radically altered their Marxist Leninist organizing practices to an assembly model.

On January 1, 1994, the EZLN launched a surprise insurrection, expelling Mexican police and wealthy landowners and declaring war on the Mexican state. Seven cities and thousands of villages were encompassed in the liberated territory, where the EZLN announced the beginning of a new system of communal self-governance. Subsequently, the system in Chiapas has blended Indigenous Mayan traditions with values and techniques from the global left. In Mayan culture, the *caracol* or snail shell is a deeply meaningful symbol of coordination between communities, each line of its shell standing for a layer in the commune of communes. In the Zapatista administration, there are five centers of political coordination. These centers draw together dozens of autonomous *municipios* that themselves map onto organic, small-scale communities and villages. Altogether, the *caracoles* system has governed a wide territory, home to somewhere between 200,000 and 300,000 inhabitants.

The *caracoles* system embodies the social-ecological principle of unity in diversity. Each *caracol* is home to Good Government Councils, which coordinate the *municipios* and mediate conflicts between communities. Each council has its own mandate, decided upon and amended by the communities that constitute it. Individual leadership roles within the Good Government Councils rotate according to these mandates once every several weeks or up to several months.[15]

Like Rojava, the Zapatista experience highlights the iterative nature of radically democratic politics. In November 2023, in the face of rising gang and cartel violence, human trafficking, and humanitarian crisis, the Zapatista Movement issued a communiqué announcing a dramatic restructuring of their political system. This included narrowing the competencies allocated at the higher levels of administration, which had proven vulnerable to corruption, and the dissolution of the autonomous municipalities. Instead of consolidating power on the heels of their victory, the Zapatistas looked to decentralize power. Zapatista Rebel Autonomous Municipalities were replaced with thousands of Local Autonomous Governments (LAGs) accountable to popular assemblies in every community of Zapatista support. The LAGs have increased powers, including establishing salaries, documenting and addressing corruption, and managing local health and education systems. At the same time, security forces were reinforced to deal with the violence, COVID-19, and the humanitarian crises of migrants seeking safe passage. The authors of a 2023 communiqué write that the Zapatista LAGs are "the core of all autonomy." The new system, the communiqué's authors admit, seems complicated: "We understand that you may have problems assimilating this. And that, for a while, you will struggle to understand it. It took us 10 years to think about it, and of those 10 years, three to prepare it for its practice."[16]

In principle, delegation is the key difference between conventional representative democracy and confederal, direct democracy. However, in practice, things are not always so clear-cut. Both the Zapatistas and Kurdish revolutionaries have struggled in their own ways to bridge the gap between ordinary people and professional administrators. In both cases, state violence, internal resistance, and the need for political education have proved to be serious obstacles and, in many ways, the fully liberated, federal society that social ecologists imagine remains a utopian ideal.

Still, a truly democratic society is not one where isolated communities live untethered from outside influences or obligations. Nor is it a world where individual communities and ecosystems are exploited for some alleged greater good. The Zapatista Movement speaks of "one world where many worlds fit." In linking Indigenous resistance movements to the anarchist traditions of the global left, both Rojava and Zapatismo show that particular struggles against racism, sexism, and other forms of hierarchy can "fit" within a broader ecumenical or "universalist" struggle. Although many questions remain about how to make the praxis of directly democratic confederalism, it is a politics that gives material reality to the truth that the particular and the universal are inextricably linked. Autonomy and freedom are ensured within an interdependent whole.

Conclusion

During Bookchin's lifetime, the global ecological crisis was primarily a threat on the horizon. Today, we are experiencing the catastrophe first hand as our biosphere rapidly declines. Climate-induced heat waves, drought, floods, and fire threaten vital crops, disrupting global supply chains and driving up the costs associated with food and basic goods. Extreme heat, storms, and fires exacerbate poverty and propel displacement of the poor and vulnerable to wealthy countries. The powerful institutions and wealthy elites responsible for this instability have only taken advantage of them for their own benefit. While poor and working people struggle to survive, corporations experience record profits. What can people of consciousness do to counteract this situation?

First, I think we must openly and insistently acknowledge how deeply these problems are embedded in our society's political and economic fabric. Capitalism, as an economic system based on endless accumulation, imperils complex ecosystems; it cannot be reformed or painted "green." The state is equally to blame for enforcing the status quo through violence as well as for insulating elites from the consequences of their own decisions. The roots of state and capitalist domination exist in all relationships of submission and command. Hierarchy as an organizing principle divides people, pitting them against each other, and enables all kinds of self-destruction. We have to cut through the Gordian knot.

But it is not enough to critique the existing system. We must begin to describe liberatory political institutions in positive terms and articulate our own understandings of freedom. Those new institutions must also have internally coherent means and ends. One of the lasting lessons of twentieth-century socialism is that without a genuine *democracy of content*, as Bookchin's mentor Josef Weber called it, promising popular movements lapse back into old authoritarian patterns and habits.

In this book, I have tried to illustrate how social-ecological movements articulate egalitarian ideals through struggle. In doing so, they present powerful models for how to tackle the polycrisis. Self-reflection, healing, and character development are foundational to this process. Through disciplines such as *hevaltî*, *tekmil*, and *perxwede*, revolutionaries fashion themselves into the kinds of people who are capable of being democratic. Self-critical muscles come into play as revolutionaries launch new democratic experiments such as the Burlington Greens, Cooperation Jackson, or Barcelona en Comú. Here, movements demonstrate that ordinary people can manage collective affairs and that communities can meet their needs in sustainable ways. In Rojava, thousands of people have lost their lives in the struggle to realize a utopian ideal. Their sacrifice demonstrates that revolutionary courage can flourish even under dire circumstances.

There is no single blueprint for a democratic and ecological way of life. Indeed, if the last decades of emancipatory social movements and democratic experimentation have revealed anything, it is that each community must reinvent real democracy for itself. The very language of "democracy" is subject to these slippery and contradictory dynamics. In many parts of the world, people strongly associate the word "democracy" with Western domination and neocolonialism. In others, democracy is the cornerstone of liberation. There may never be definitive solutions to conflicting interpretations of liberation. What matters, I think, is to maintain a stance of openness and inquiry because no individual or movement has all the answers.

Nor are there easy answers to the dilemmas at the messy and complicated intersection of theory and practice. Experiments rarely function the way we expect them to. On this topic, I often find myself returning to the municipalist activist's metaphor of sandpipers. We are on the beach, chasing powerful waves that swell and crash, only to break and recede just as quickly as they arrive. The sand beneath our feet can feel hard and impenetrable. But on certain days, one looks at the beach to discover that the dunes have shifted and the terrain is new.

Every attempt at face-to-face decision-making enhances the meaning and possibilities of revolution. In this way, political experiments are successful even when they do not "succeed." We do not often think of "revolution" as having a history, but two and a half centuries ago, the word pertained solely to the field of physics, where it described the trajectory of objects along a recurring path.[1] Conservative backlash after the French Revolution led to the term taking on a new meaning as former participants in the uprising demanded a return to its original, emancipatory spirit. In pushing society forward, revolutionaries gesture back. Stateless societies past and present provide a wealth of historical models from which people of consciousness can construct a radical alternative modernity. Our task is not to rehabilitate the past but to move forward with lessons in hand.

It is not an accident that a democratic awakening is taking place across the world just as our planet is experiencing a global ecological crisis. Political scientists often think of democracy as a set of institutions and practices, but it is really a way of treating each other. When the Haudenosaunee take a moment before their assemblies to acknowledge plants, animals, and minerals in creation, it is not an empty gesture. In a literal sense, they are involving nature in a great cosmic unfolding of collective reason. When activists in Jinwar rehabilitate plant-based medicine of the Mesopotamia region, they contribute to that evolutionary process. Or when permaculture practitioners show schoolchildren how to plant wetland grasses in a waterlogged lawn, they are contributing to that evolutionary process as well. The comrades whose stories appear in this book demonstrate profound courage. As global average temperatures climb, it can be tempting to give in to despair. Their perseverance speaks to a resilience and love of freedom embedded in nature itself. Reconciliation with nature is, at the end of the day, a reconciliation with ourselves.

Recommended Reading

Bookchin, M. (1991) *The Ecology of Freedom: The Emergence and Dissolution of Hierarchy.* Montréal: Black Rose Books.

Bookchin, M, (2015) *The Next Revolution: Popular Assemblies and the Promise of Direct Democracy.* Edited by Blair Taylor and Debbie Bookchin. New York: Verso Books.

Bookchin, M. (2021) *From Urbanization to Cities: The Politics of Democratic Municipalism.* Chico, CA: AK Press.

Bookchin, M. (2023) *Remaking Society: A New Ecological Politics.* Chico, CA: AK Press.

Chodorkoff, D. (2014) *Anthropology of Utopia.* Porsgrunn, Norway: New Compass Press.

Dirik, D. (2021) *The Kurdish Women's Movement: History, Theory, Practice.* London: Pluto Press.

Graeber, D. (2013) *The Democracy Project: A History, a Crisis, a Movement.* New York: Spiegel & Grau.

Graeber, D. and Wengrow, D. (2021) *The Dawn of Everything: A New History of Humanity.* New York: Farrar, Straus, and Giroux.

Heller, C. (1999) *Ecology of Everyday Life: Rethinking the Desire for Nature.* Montréal: Black Rose Books.

Kadalie, M. (2022) *Intimate Direct Democracy: Fort Mose, the Great Dismal Swamp, and the Human Quest for Freedom.* Atlanta, GA: On Our Own Authority! Publishing.

Kadalie, M. and Zonneveld, A. (2019) *Pan-African Social Ecology: Speeches, Conversations, and Essays.* Atlanta, GA: On Our Own Authority! Publishing.

Maeckelbergh, M. (2009) *The Will of the Many: How the Alterglobalisation Movement Is Changing the Face of Democracy.* London: Pluto Press.

Milstein, C. (2020) *Deciding for Ourselves: The Promise of Direct Democracy*. Chico, CA: AK Press.

Monticelli, L. (2022). *The Future Is Now: An Introduction to Prefigurative Politics*. Bristol: Bristol University Press.

Öcalan, A. and Graeber, D. (2015) *Manifesto for a Democratic Civilization*, Vol. 1, international initiative edition. Porsgrunn, Norway: New Compass Press.

Price, A. (2023) *Recovering Bookchin: Social Ecology and the Crises of Our Time*. Chico, CA: AK Press.

Sitrin, M. (2006) *Horizontalism: Voices of Popular Power in Argentina*. Oakland, CA: AK Press.

Tokar, B. (1994) *The Green Alternative: Creating an Ecological Future*. San Pedro, CA: R. and E. Miles.

White, D. (2015) *Bookchin: A Critical Appraisal*. London: Pluto Press.

Notes

INTRODUCTION

1. Chodorkoff, D. (2001) "Editorial," *Harbinger*, 2(1), October 1. https://social-ecology.org/wp/2001/10/harbinger-vol-2-no-1-editorial/.
2. Biehl, J. (2015) *Ecology or Catastrophe: The Life of Murray Bookchin*. New York: Oxford University Press.
3. White, D. F. (2015) *Bookchin: A Critical Appraisal*. London: Pluto Press; Price, A. (2023) *Recovering Bookchin: Social Ecology and the Crises of Our Time*. Chico, CA: AK Press.

CHAPTER 1

1. Morin, E. (1999) *Homeland Earth: A Manifesto for the New Millennium*. Cresskill, NJ: Hampton Press.
2. Akuno, K., Drolet, B., and Norberg, D. (2021) "Shifting Focus," The Anarchist Library, November 1. https://theanarchistlibrary.org/library/kali-akuno-brian-drolet-doug-norberg-shifting-focus.
3. Bookchin, M. (2007) *Social Ecology and Communalism*. Oakland, CA: AK Press, 19.
4. Reclus, E. (2013) *Anarchy, Geography, Modernity: Selected Writings of Elisée Reclus*. Edited by Clark John and Camille Martin. Binghampton, NY: PM Press.
5. Nelson, A. (2024) "Marx, Work, Agency and Postcapitalist Prefiguration," *Human Geography*, March. https://doi.org/10.1177/19427786241237434.
6. Wright, D., Camden-Pratt, C., and Hill, S. (2011) *Social Ecology Applying Ecological Understanding to Our Lives and Our Planet*. Stroud: Hawthorne Press.

7. Ibid.
8. Pfretzschner, P. A. (1955) "Book Reviews: Community and Environment, a Discourse on Social Ecology, by E. A. Gutkind," *Western Political Quarterly*, 8(1), 140–1.
9. School of Social Ecology, UC Irvine. https://uci.edu/academics/social-ecology.php.
10. Hill, S. B. (n.d.) "What Is Social Ecology?" www.zulenet.com/see/newStuartHill.html.
11. Hill, S. B. (n.d.) *Social Ecology for Educators*. www.stuartbhill.com/index.php/social-ecology-for-educators.
12. US Solidarity Economy Network. https://ussen.org/.
13. Enzinna, W. (2015) "A Dream of Secular Utopia in ISIS's Backyard," *New York Times*, 24 November. www.nytimes.com/2015/11/29/magazine/a-dream-of-utopia-in-hell.html.
14. Öcalan, A. (2017) *Democratic Confederalism*, 4th ed. Cologne: International Initiative Edition, 26.
15. Zibechi, R. (2013) *Territories in Resistance: A Cartography of Latin American Social Movements*. Oakland, CA: AK Press.
16. De La Cadena, M. (2010) "Indigenous Cosmopolitics in the Andes: Conceptual Reflections beyond 'Politics,'" *Cultural Anthropology*, 25(2), 334–70; Escobar, A. (2020) *Pluriversal Politics: The Real and the Possible*. Durham, NC: Duke University Press.

CHAPTER 2

1. Godfrey-Smith, P. (2016) *Other Minds: The Octopus, the Sea, and the Deep Origins of Consciousness*. New York: Farrar, Straus and Giroux, 12.
2. Heller, C. (1999) *The Ecology of Everyday Life: Rethinking the Desire for Nature*. Montréal: Black Rose Books.
3. Godfrey-Smith, *Other Minds*, 19.

4. Kropotkin, P. A., Bonzo, N. O., Graeber, D., Grubačić, A., Kinna, R., Antliff, A., and GATS (2021) *Mutual Aid: An Illuminated Factor of Evolution*. Oakland, CA: PM Press.

5. Trosper, R. L. (2022) *Indigenous Economics: Sustaining Peoples and Their Lands*. Tucson: University of Arizona Press.

6. Hestad, D. and Recio, E. (2022) *Indigenous Peoples: Defending an Environment for All*. Policy Brief 36. Geneva: International Institute for Sustainable Development. www.iisd.org/articles/deep-dive/indigenous-peoples-defending-environment-all.

7. Ross, K. (2015) *Communal Luxury: The Political Imaginary of the Paris Commune*. London: Verso, 137.

8. Saitō, K. (2017) *Karl Marx's Ecosocialism: Capitalism, Nature, and the Unfinished Critique of Political Economy*. New York: Monthly Review Press.

9. Pearce, F. (2015) "Global Extinction Rates: Why Do Estimates Vary So Wildly?" *Yale Environment 360*, August 17. https://e360.yale.edu/features/global_extinction_rates_why_do_estimates_vary_so_wildly.

10. Elhacham, E. et al. (2020) "Global Human-Made Mass Exceeds All Living Biomass," *Nature*, 588(7838), 442–4.

11. Benja, F. and Scott, E. (2024) "Taylor Swift and the Top Polluters Department," *Carbon Market Watch*, February 13. https://carbonmarketwatch.org/2024/02/13/taylor-swift-and-the-top-polluters-department/.

12. Bookchin, M. (2007) *Social Ecology and Communalism*. Oakland, CA. Edinburgh: AK Press, 42–3.

13. Crawford, N. (2019) "Pentagon Fuel Use, Climate Change, and the Costs of War," Watson Institute for International and Public Affairs, Brown University. https://watson.brown.edu/costsofwar/papers/ClimateChangeandCostofWar.

14. Ortner, S. B. (2010) *Making Gender: The Politics and Erotics of Culture*. Boston: Beacon Press.

15. Graeber, D. and Wengrow, D. (2021) *The Dawn of Everything: A New History of Humanity*. New York: Farrar, Straus and Giroux, 119.

16. Bookchin, M. (1986) *The Modern Crisis*. Philadelphia: New Society Publishers, 54.

17. Bookchin, M. (2004) *Post-scarcity Anarchism*, 3rd ed. Oakland, CA: AK Press, 102.

18. Council, S. (2024) "SF Exec Defends 'brutal' Trend: Lay off Staff to Free Cash for AI," *SF Gate*, April 17. www.sfgate.com/tech/article/lay-off-workers-for-ai-investment-19408308.php.

19. Schmelzer, M., Vetter, A., and Vansintjan, A. (2022) *The Future Is Degrowth: A Guide to a World beyond Capitalism*. London: Verso Books.

20. Horn-Miller, K. (2013) "What Does Indigenous Participatory Democracy Look Like? Kahnawà:Ke's Community Decision Making Process," *Review of Constitutional Studies*, 18(1). https://ssrn.com/abstract=2437675.

21. Kimmerer, R. W. (2013) *Braiding Sweetgrass: Indigenous Wisdom, Scientific Knowledge and the Teachings of Plants*. Minneapolis: Milkweed Editions, 140.

22. Butler, J. (2015) *Notes toward a Performative Theory of Assembly*. Cambridge, MA: Harvard University Press, 21.

23. Ibid.

24. Beard, S. et al. (2024) "Racism as a Public Health Issue in Environmental Health Disparities and Environmental Justice: Working toward Solutions." *Environmental Health*, 23(1), 8.

25. Proudhon, P.-J. (2022) "Principles of the Philosophy of Progress," The Anarchist Library, December 4. https://theanarchistlibrary.org/library/pierre-joseph-proudhon-principles-of-the-philosophy-of-progress.

26. Bookchin, M, (2015) *The Next Revolution: Popular Assemblies and the Promise of Direct Democracy*. Edited by Blair Taylor and Debbie Bookchin. New York: Verso Books.

27. Kadalie, M. and Zonneveld, A. (2019) *Pan-African Social Ecology: Speeches, Conversations, and Essays*. Atlanta, GA: On Our Own Authority! Publishing.

28. Kadalie, M. (2022) *Intimate Direct Democracy: Fort Mose, the Great Dismal Swamp, and the Human Quest for Freedom*. Atlanta, GA: On Our Own Authority! Publishing.

CHAPTER 3

1. hooks, b. (2009) *Belonging: A Culture of Place*. London: Routledge, 177.

2. Clark, A. (n.d.) "Vernon A.M.E. Church Continues Its Mission 100 Years after the Tulsa Race Massacre," National Trust for Historic Preservation. https://savingplaces.org/stories/vernon-ame-church-continues-its-mission-100-years-after-the-tulsa-race-massacre.

3. Nembhard, G. (2014) *Collective Courage: A History of African American Cooperative Economic Thought and Practice*. University Park: Pennsylvania State University Press, 86.

4. Van De Sande, M. (2013) "The Prefigurative Politics of Tahrir Square: An Alternative Perspective on the 2011 Revolutions," *Res Publica*, 19(3), 223–39.

5. Bookchin, M. (1969) *A Note on Affinity Groups*. The Anarchist Library. https://theanarchistlibrary.org/library/murray-bookchin-a-note-on-affinity-groups.

6. Ibid.

7. Guneser, H. and Finley, E. (2019) "The Evolution of the Kurdish Paradigm," in *Social Ecology and Right to the City*, edited by F. Venturini, E. Degirmenci, and I. Morales. Montreal: Black Rose Books.

8. Cansız, S. (2019) *Sara: Prison Memoir of a Kurdish Revolutionary*, translated by J. Biehl. London: Pluto Press.

9. Dirik, D. (2021) *The Kurdish Women's Movement: History, Theory, Practice*. London: Pluto Press, 84.

10. Arendt, H. and Kohn, J. (2005) *The Promise of Politics*. New York: Schoken Books, 93.

11. Ross, L. (Forthcoming) *Calling In*. New York: Simon & Schuster.
12. Boggs, J. and Boggs, G. L. (1969) *Revolution and Evolution in the Twentieth Century*. New York: Monthly Review Press.
13. Bancroft, L. (2002) *Why Does He Do That? Inside the Minds of Angry and Controlling Men*. New York: Berkley Books.

CHAPTER 4

1. Sankaran, V. (2024) "Sumatran Orangutan Seen Treating Wound with Traditional Plant Medicine in First for Wild Animals," *The Independent*, May 3. www.independent. co.uk/news/science/orangutan-wounded-medicine-plant-leaves-b2538950.html.
2. Kimmerer, R. W. (2013) *Braiding Sweetgrass: Indigenous Wisdom, Scientific Knowledge and the Teachings of Plants*. Minneapolis: Milkweed Editions, 473.
3. Holmgren, D. (2018) *RetroSuburbia: The Downshifter's Guide to a Resilient Future*. Seymour, Australia: Melliodora Publishing.
4. Alexander, S. and Gleeson, B. (2019) *Degrowth in the Suburbs: A Radical Urban Imaginary*. Singapore: Springer Nature.
5. Dirik, D. (2021) *The Kurdish Women's Movement: History, Theory, Practice*. London: Pluto Press, 77.
6. Akkaya, A. H. and Jongerden, J. (2012) "Reassembling the Political: The PKK and the Project of Radical Democracy," *European Journal of Turkish Studies* 14. https://doi.org/10.4000/ejts.4615.
7. Court, M. and Den Hond, C. (n.d.) "Is This the End of Rojava?" *The Nation*. www.thenation.com/article/world/rojava-kurds-syria/.
8. Yıldırım, U. (2024) "Decolonial Ecologies and 'Low-Intensity War' in Kurdistan," *Middle East Report*, 113 (July). https://merip.org/2024/07/decolonial-ecologies-and-low-intensity-war-in-kurdistan/.

CHAPTER 5

1. Robert, H. M., Robert, S. C., Robert, H. M., Evans, W. J., Honemann, D. H., Balch, T. J., Seabold, D. E., and Gerber, S. (2020) *Robert's Rules of Order Newly Revised*, 12th ed. New York: Public Affairs.

2. Keane, J. (2009) *The Life and Death of Democracy*. New York: W.W. Norton & Co, 4.

3. Ibid., 132

4. Ibid., 120.

5. Luxemburg, R., Hudis, P., and Anderson, K. (2004) *The Rosa Luxemburg Reader*. New York: Monthly Review Press.

6. Mbah, S. and Igariwey, I. E. (1997) *African Anarchism: The History of a Movement*. Tucson, AZ: See Sharp Press, 36.

7. Martin, G. (2012) *African Political Thought*. New York: Palgrave Macmillan, 16.

8. Dubois, L. (2005) *Avengers of the New World: The Story of the Haitian Revolution*. Cambridge, MA: The Belknap Press of Harvard University Press, 100.

9. Kadalie, M. and Zonneveld, A. (2019) *Pan-African Social Ecology: Speeches, Conversations, and Essays*. Atlanta, GA: On Our Own Authority! Publishing.

10. Mbah and Igariwey, *African Anarchism*, 49.

11. Gesley, J. (2021) "50 Years of Women's Suffrage in Switzerland," *Library of Congress Blogs*, April 28. https://blogs.loc.gov/law/2021/04/50-years-of-womens-suffrage-in-switzerland.

12. Rojava Information Center (2019) "Beyond the Frontlines: The Building of the Democratic System in North and East Syria." https://rojavainformationcenter.org/2019/12/report-beyond-the-frontlines/.

13. Bruinessen, M. van. (1992) *Agha, Shaikh and State: The Social and Political Structures of Kurdistan*. London: Zed Books.

14. Rojava Information Center (2023) "DAANES' Social Contract, 2023 Edition." https://rojavainformationcenter.org/2023/12/aanes-social-contract-2023-edition/.
15. Habiba, A. (2011) "How People of Color Occupy Wall Street," *The Nation*. www.thenation.com/article/archive/how-people-color-occupy-wall-street/.
16. Bookchin, M. (2021) *From Urbanization to Cities: The Politics of Democratic Municipalism*. Chico, CA: AK Press.
17. Rubio-Pueyo, V. (2017) *Municipalism in Spain: From Barcelona to Madrid, and beyond*. New York: Rosa Luxemburg Stiftung, 4.
18. Engler, M. and Engler, P. (2023) "Lessons from Barcelona's 8-Year Experiment in Radical Governance," *Waging Nonviolence*, May 9. https://wagingnonviolence.org/2023/05/lessons-barcelona-en-comu-ada-colau/.
19. Shaner, A. (2022) "IMZ: 10 Years of Citizens Assemblies," *ZNetwork*, December 5. https://znetwork.org/znetarticle/imz-10-years-of-citizens-assemblies/.
20. Bookchin, D. (2019) "The Future We Deserve" in *Fearless Cities: A Guide to the Global Municipalist Movement*, edited by Barcelona En Comú. Oxford: New Internationalist Publications, Ltd.
21. Akuno, K., Meyer, M., and Wolff, R. D. (eds.) (2023) *Jackson Rising Redux: Lessons on Building the Future in the Present*. Oakland, CA: PM Press.
22. Kolokotronis, A. (n.d.) "Municipalist Syndicalism: Organizing the New Working Class," *ROAR Magazine*. https://roarmag.org/essays/municipalist-syndicalism-alex-kolokotronis/.

CHAPTER 6

1. Razsa, M. (2015) *Bastards of Utopia: Living Radical Politics after Socialism*. Bloomington: Indiana University Press.
2. Howe, J. (1986) *The Kuna Gathering: Contemporary Village Politics in Panama*. Austin: University of Texas Press.

3. Human Rights Watch (2006) *"Genocide in Iraq": The Anfal Campaign against the Kurds.* www.hrw.org/report/2006/08/14/genocide-iraq-anfal-campaign-against-kurds/report-summary.

4. Kadalie, M. and Zonneveld, A. (2019) *Pan-African Social Ecology: Speeches, Conversations, and Essays.* Atlanta, GA: On Our Own Authority! Publishing.

5. Mohammed, K. and Kadalie, M. (n.d.) *Organization and Spontaneity: The Theory of the Vanguard Party and Its Application to the Black Movement in the US Today.* Atlanta, GA: On Our Own Authority! Publishing.

6. Kadalie and Zonneveld, *Pan-African Social Ecology.*

7. Fondation-Institut Kurde de Paris (2017) *The Kurdish Population,* Institutkurde.org, January 12. www.institutkurde.org/en/info/the-kurdish-population-1232551004.

8. Öcalan, A. (2017) *Democratic Nation,* 2nd ed. Cologne: International Initiative.

9. Eliassi, B. (2014) "Nationalism, Cosmopolitanism and Statelessness: An Interview with Craig Calhoun," *Kurdish Studies,* 2(1), 61–74.

10. Rojava Information Center (2023) "DAANES' Social Contract, 2023 Edition." https://rojavainformationcenter.org/2023/12/aanes-social-contract-2023-edition/.

11. Rojava Information Center (2019) "Beyond the Frontlines: The Building of the Democratic System in North and East Syria." https://rojavainformationcenter.org/2019/12/report-beyond-the-frontlines/.

12. Finley, E. and Demirbaş, A. (2016) "Sur: A Neighbourhood of History, Hope, and Resistance." *Uneven Earth,* 23 July. https://unevenearth.org/2016/07/sur-a-neighbourhood-of-history-hope-and-resistance/.

13. Council of Europe (2015) "Annual Report 2014 of the European Court of Human Rights, Council of Europe." www.coe.int/en/web/execution/annual-reports.

14. De La Cadena, M. (2010) "Indigenous Cosmopolitics in the Andes: Conceptual Reflections beyond 'Politics,'" *Cultural Anthropology*, 25(2), 334–70.

15. Oikonomakis, L. (2015) "Why We Still Love the Zapatistas," *ROAR Magazine*. https://roarmag.org/magazine/why-we-still-love-the-zapatistas/.

16. Enlace Zapatista (2023) "Ninth Part: The New Structure of Zapastista Autonomy," *Enlace Zapatista*, 14 November. https://enlacezapatista.ezln.org.mx/2023/11/13/ninth-part-the-new-structure-of-zapastista-autonomy/.

CONCLUSION

1. Baker, K. M. and Edelstein, D. (2015) *Scripting Revolution: A Historical Approach to the Comparative Study of Revolutions*. Stanford, CA: Stanford University Press.

Index

Thanks to our Patreon subscriber:

Ciaran Kane

Who has shown generosity and
comradeship in support of our publishing.

Check out the other perks you get by subscribing
to our Patreon – visit patreon.com/plutopress.

Subscriptions start from £3 a month.

The Pluto Press Newsletter

Hello friend of Pluto!

Want to stay on top of the best radical books
we publish?

Then sign up to be the first to hear about our
new books, as well as special events,
podcasts and videos.

You'll also get 50% off your first order with us
when you sign up.

Come and join us!

Go to bit.ly/PlutoNewsletter